Miles Ahead

---ᴏᴏᴏ---

DEVOTIONS FROM OLDER ADULTS

EDITED BY
CAROL SPARGO PIERSKALLA

JUDSON PRESS
VALLEY FORGE

Miles Ahead: Devotions from Older Adults
© 2001 by Judson Press, Valley Forge, PA 19482-0851
All rights reserved.

Scripture quotations in this volume are from the following versions of the Bible:

The New Revised Standard Version of the Bible, copyright © 1989 by the Division of Christian Education of the National Council of the Churches of Christ in the United States of America. Used by permission. All rights reserved (NRSV).

HOLY BIBLE: New International Version, copyright © 1973, 1978, 1984. Used by permission of Zondervan Bible Publishers (NIV).

The New King James Version. Copyright © 1972, 1984 by Thomas Nelson Inc. (NKJV).

The Holy Bible, New Century Version, copyright © 1987, 1988, 1991 by Word Publishing, Nashville, TN 37214. Used by permission (NCV).

The Holy Bible, King James Version (KJV).

The New American Bible, copyright © 1970, 1986, 1991 by the Confraternity of Christian Doctrine, 3211 Fourth Street, N.E., Washington, D.C. 20017. All rights reserved (NAB).

The Living Bible, copyright © 1971. Used by permission of Tyndale House Publishers, Inc. Wheaton, IL 60189. All rights reserved (TLB).

The Revised Standard Version of the Bible, copyright © 1946, 1952, 1971, by the Division of Christian Education of the National Council of the Churches of Christ in the U.S.A. Used by permission (RSV).

The Contemporary English Version. Copyright © 1991, 1992, 1995 by American Bible Society. Used by permission (CEV).

The New English Bible, Copyright © The Delegates of the Oxford University Press and The Syndics of the Cambridge University Press 1961, 1970. (NEB)

Library of Congress Cataloging-in-Publication Data

Miles ahead : devotions from older adults / edited by Carol Spargo Pierskalla.

    p. cm.
    Includes index.
    ISBN 0-8170-1405-5 (pbk. : alk. paper)
    1. Christian aged—Prayer-books and devotions—English. I. Pierskalla, Carol Spargo.

BV4580 .M53 2001
242'.65—dc21   2001038134

Printed in Canada

07 06 05 04 03 02 01

10 9 8 7 6 5 4 3 2 1

Miles Ahead

To Emma Lou Benignus
whose life and faith
have been an inspiration
to young and old alike

and

To the faithful pilgrims
who contributed to this book

Contents

———

Preface

On December 25, 2000, I began the sixty-sixth year of my life. With this event came a feeling of adventure, of newness and joy. There is nothing God-given about making a change at age sixty-five—yet I feel different. I feel on the verge of wondrous spiritual happenings. As I write this I am sitting in my cabin on Three Island Lake in northern Minnesota, looking out on a frozen white landscape. Each morning I watch in wonder as a new day dawns and life unfolds, sometimes in joy, sometimes in sorrow, but always in God.

In 1999 Judson Press called me to discuss a book of devotions by and for older adults. We decided we wanted devotions that would uplift and inform, that older adults could relate to at many levels. And we wanted to include people from various Christian traditions in order to give our readers the benefit of diverse theological viewpoints. So we sent out requests for contributions to several hundred persons and asked them for their own reflections. We encouraged multiple submissions because we recognized that so many years of living give birth to more insights than a single volume can hope to hold. Editing these submissions has been uplifting for me, and I'm sure some of them will speak to you as well.

If you enjoy this book and if it sparked some memory or wisdom you want to share, please write to me care of Judson Press. I will enjoy hearing from you.

Carol Spargo Pierskalla
"Sunrise" on Three Island Lake
Bemidji, Minnesota
January 2001

LONNIE LANE

On-the-Job Training

PROLOGUE

Then those who revered the Lord spoke with one
another. The LORD took note and listened, and a
book of remembrance was written before him of
those who revered the LORD and thought on his name.
(Malachi 3:16, NRSV)

As part of my work at Judson Press, it was my job to put in
order the devotionals to be included in this book you hold
in your hands. As I read through manuscripts, typed
some, or reformatted others from the computer discs the
authors sent in with their submissions, I began to realize I
have a lot more in common with these older adults than I
realized. Okay, I know I'm a grandmother several times
over; I know that when I take my mother to the movies we

can now both get in at the senior discount price; I know that several years ago my very own subscription to *Modern Maturity* suddenly appeared in my mailbox right after my fiftieth birthday. (How do they know?) But I didn't really consider that I was one of those folks called older adults.

Yet as I read of the memories shared and the struggles overcome, I identified with them so closely I had to stifle an impulse to write to many of the contributors and say, "Hey, I know just what you mean. Me, too."

Through these writings I found a new sense of courage and a grace-filled acceptance of God's timetable in our lives and the changes that inevitably come, a grace and courage that shone forth from the pages to me as I worked with them. May this be your experience as you read.

Lord, grant the same strengthening and blessings you granted to me to all those who read through these treasures of life experiences. Remind us to say a prayer for each of the writers as we read their stories—to bless them back for sharing with the rest of us. Amen.

SECTION ONE

Reflections from the Years

CAROL SPARGO PIERSKALLA

The River's Run

A PARABLE

I like being my age. I like not getting up for work every morning. I like having time to sit up in bed with my coffee, my spiritual readings, and prayers. I like the time I have to spend with my family and friends.

But then comes that middle-of-the-night panic attack, during which I wonder how many years of health and vigor I have left, and fear creeps in. I remember hearing about a woman whose husband was dying from cancer. She said she woke up beside him every night thinking, "He's dying, and I can do nothing to stop it!"

Yes, I'm growing older, and nothing can stop that. And yes, while growing older has its pluses (as Barbara Smith tallies in "Checking the Lists"), aging is not a concept that most of us welcome, especially when it involves physical deterioration and illness. In struggling to find a positive metaphor for aging, I chose the river because of its life-giving image! The river gives me a sense of the power and meaning in my life. Perhaps it will do the same for you.

Far to the West, where lives the Source of all Life, a spring bubbled up high in the mountains on rocky ground above the tree line. Some of her life seeped into the ground, but most of it flowed over the rocks and away down the mountain, carving a path between trees and rocks, rushing turbulently in headlong flight to reach flat and level ground. Here she attracted the strong and venturesome souls, the kayakers, the white water paddlers, those whose adventurous spirit matched hers. As she reached the foothills, her speed slowed, and she picked up flycasters and birdwatchers. Deer, raccoons, and otters lived near her banks, relying on her life source.

But it was when she reached the flat land that she really came into her own. Here she became the Source, for all life flowed from her banks. Villages, towns, and cities sprang up on her shores. Ships of all sizes, from canoes to barges to ocean liners, found their way to her. She was the center of life, and the world belonged to her. She swelled and shrank depending on the season, but at no time did she disappear or disappoint the confidence placed in her.

Eventually she left the shipping, the commotion, the pollution of the human habitations behind her. The high banks and cliffs melted into indistinct marshes as she entered the wetlands. Now she birthed the wild things, the flying and crawling creatures that depended on her lifegiving liquid. She experienced the nest building, egg laying, and hatching of ducks, geese, and sandpipers. She watched as beaver kits emerged from their lodges to swim and frolic. She was part of this creation and deep, inner swells of fulfillment and satisfaction coursed through her as she spread out to encompass these lowlands.

But this spreading and nurturing took its toll and by the time she had passed through the wetlands and into the dry country, her strength had dwindled to a trickle, hardly deep enough to wet the feet of those who crossed her. She felt calm and unhurried, enjoying the sunshine, the occasional rain, the visits of dry country creatures who relied on her still.

As the days wore on, the rain came less frequently, the

flow became a trickle and anxiety turned to actual fear. Was this how it was to end, a trickle in the desert, her life slowly seeping away to nothingness? Fear and loneliness overcame her.

One day she became aware of a new sound, a rushing noise in the background. It had come upon her so slowly that she had been unaware of it. She turned a corner and found herself tumbling downhill toward a chasm in the ground. With what little strength she had left, she pushed off the edge and flew through the air, a tiny waterfall. At the bottom of the chasm, she fell to a mighty river, one that revived her with its fresh coldness, its boundless energy. She should have been frightened but she felt confident and secure. She should have been tired, but she felt rejuvenated. It felt familiar, comfortable, even joyful.

Eventually she recognized that this was one of her many daughters, sprung from her own life back in the mountains. She would flow on now, a part of this new life, and both would join yet another daughter or sister, until they eventually emptied into the great oceans to become a part of its teeming, lifegiving waters.

Some days she longed to set her own course again, to be the center of activity and growth that she had once been. It had been a good time. Sometimes she longed for the wetlands, for the harsh, yet often tender life she witnessed there. But mostly she was content, her fears at rest. She relaxed, letting Daughter River carry her, knowing that eventually they would both find themselves back home, joined once again to the Source of all Life, under the mountains, far to the West.

———◦◦◦———

Cogitation

No eye has seen, nor ear heard, nor the human heart conceived, what God has prepared for those who love him. (1 Corinthians 2:9, NRSV)

Receiving the gift of a long, healthy life gives one the pleasure of looking back over the highlights of life along the way. At the moment of any event, we may not realize the connotation of a deeper meaning in what we have learned—until years later. We need time to reflect. Jesus said, "Seeing they see not, hearing they hear not." In some cases one may never hear, see, or understand, but an example of belated learning follows.

Mom was our first science teacher. Our leisurely walks in the woods and around the lake, in the company of a constant menagerie of pets, taught my sister, Elsie, and me many lifelong lessons.

One morning on one of our walks, we found a number of tadpoles. We took some of them home and watched them develop over time into handsome bullfrogs. Of course, then we turned them loose in a nearly pond to listen to their music.

On another day, at another time, we gathered a couple ugly-looking worms. Mom saw their potential. At her urging, we put these worms in a big cardboard box and watched them gorge themselves on leaves until they became plump and lazy. Soon, they each tucked themselves into a gray cocoon. Time passed and eventually those worms (caterpillars, Mom taught us) burst form from their pupa stage as beautiful butterflies.

While those "worms" were crawling around in the dirt, looking for something to eat, they had no vision for their future. When those tadpoles were swimming aimlessly in the murky water, they had no concept of what they would become. Of course, tadpoles and caterpillars don't have conscious thought—at least, I don't think they do!

But so it is with God's plan for our lives. We do not understand our designated road of ups and downs, twists and turns. Like the tadpole and the caterpillars, we don't give it much, if any, thought. We are too busy looking for our next meal or for the funds to pay the bills. Yet, God has a plan for our lives. We need to listen to the Holy Spirit for some whisper of how our future will transform us from a slimy tadpole or a wormlike caterpillar—into a handsome bullfrog or a lovely butterfly.

We may not know what our future will take shape, but we can be certain that our transformation in that afterlife will be permanent and wonderful. The Word says so: "We will be like him, for we will see him as he is" (1 John 3:2, NRSV). Seeing the Lord's creatures on this earth and witnessing their transformation, we can believe and know that what God's Word says is true.

Thank you, Lord, for these our lives and for the immeasurable promises in our future.

———✧✧✧———

Abundant Living

"I have come that they may have life, and that they may have it more abundantly." (John 10:10, NKJV)

One day a friend of mine asked me what I was doing. I proceeded to tell him about what my children were doing. Suddenly he stopped me in midsentence, saying, "Wait a minute. I asked what *you* were doing." My life had always been their life. I had never thought about my life.

My children were no longer home, yet I was still living my life through them. I seemed to have no life of my own. I told my friend what I was doing professionally and personally, then added, "I figure I will peak in the next twenty years, and I want to be ready." He smiled as he said, "I don't think you'll ever peak. You'll just go on and on."

I thought about what he had said on the way home. He was right. I had never looked at my life that way before. If I

10

focused on hitting peaks in my life, then there would be a downside. I wanted that abundant life Jesus talked about—the kind of life that gets better year after year. I believe that God made me in his image for his glory, and God wants me to be all I can be … for him. Years were never mentioned in that abundant life. The world talks about hitting your peak. God talks about abundant living.

I now view life as a spiritual journey, not an uphill climb toward a peak. This journey brings new lessons every day. With the lessons come blessings. My tennis game may be a little slower, but no one could enjoy it more. My glasses may have bifocals, but I see the sparkling eyes of my precious grandchildren just fine.

My friend didn't know how right he was. I am unlimited … there is no peak. God's love grows each day, and with it comes abundance. Years are merely milestones along my journey. I choose to live each day in abundance.

God, I offer my gratitude for the abundance in my life. You have given me many blessings. Each day is filled. I know that I will share these abundant days with you forever. Amen.

———⦅∕∕∕⦆———

Lighten Your Load

"If you wish to be perfect, go, sell your possessions, and give the money to the poor, and you will have treasure in heaven; then come, follow me." When the young man heard this word, he went away grieving, for he had many possessions. (Matthew 19:21-22, NRSV)

A month's delay in my retirement plans left my husband and me with three weeks to pack up or dispose of the contents of the home in which we lived for thirty years. A family of five accumulates an incredible amount of stuff. Some of our children's things were packed away in sheds, closets, and the crawl space. A yard sale reduced the volume slightly, but we still had countless odds and ends we had not used in years. We needed help to get ready to move.

In recent years, the philosophy of the Shaker sect has inspired us to try to enrich our lives by simplifying our environment. The Shakers' possessions were functional, simply designed, and beautiful. Their tools decorated their space and were shared within the community. They rarely owned anything that did not serve a useful purpose, so they had less to care for and more time to be meditative and productive. At this stage of our lives, it seems right to us to be content with fewer possessions and to have more time for people and for reflection. We planned our retirement home with this in mind. It is streamlined, with fewer rooms and nooks and crannies in which to stash things. We want to limit ourselves to the essentials, but it is not easy.

I was eager to collect things when I was a young woman. I love neatness and order, but I enjoyed decorative items that made our house seem more like home. I bought few things because our resources were limited, but people gave gifts. Before I knew it, we had more pretty (and not-so-pretty) things than we had places to put them. We started filling boxes and building closets.

Most of us tend to save too much. My husband and I have resolved to relieve each other and our children of the burden of disposing of decades of accumulation. This is an ongoing process for us. We have not yet reached our goal, but we are working at it steadily. Neatness and order are easier to achieve now. Our rooms seem more spacious because they are uncluttered. Guests are comfortable in our home, and we feel freer and more relaxed. Passing useful possessions along to others who truly need and appreciate them increases our joy as it lightens our load.

Precious Savior, help us to remember your words to us: "Take care! Be on your guard against all kinds of greed; for one's life does not consist in the abundance of possessions." (Luke 12:15, NRSV)

M. DOSIA CARLSON

—◦◦◦—

Pride and Humility

The fear of the Lord is instruction in wisdom,
and humility goes before honor.
(Proverbs 15:33, NRSV)

Why did I keep those plaques up so long? During my twenty-five years of ministry in Phoenix, Arizona, various organizations honored me with awards mounted on wooden plaques.

I eagerly hung those plaques on my office wall. Sometimes I tried to rationalize this tendency toward exhibitionism by telling myself that I owed it to the givers to display their gift. But when I became more honest with myself, I realized that I was wallowing in an unhealthy kind of pride. I was worshiping myself, not the God who created me.

After various medals and plaques had been decorating my church office for nearly twenty years, I began feeling

15

embarrassed about this display. What kind of message was I sending to people who came to see me? I felt weighed down by self-centered ostentation. Yet I hesitated to pull down the trophies and store them away.

Thank God at a journaling retreat I gained a fresh perspective on my egotistical problem. Our retreat leader invited us to engage in a meditative walk.

Participants in this spiritual discipline become keenly aware of surroundings while moving with extremely slow, deliberate steps. As a result of polio I use crutches and braces, so this "creeping" meditation felt welcome to me.

At first, as I took tiny steps on a dirt road in the desert, I found satisfaction noting little bugs I'd overlooked before. Even the shadow of my body fascinated me. But then, as a complete surprise, lines of a sturdy hymn popped into my mind: "When in our music God is glorified and adoration leaves no room for pride … "* Those words stabbed my consciousness with a message I'll never forget. I was glorifying and adoring myself, not God! What a turning away from my Creator!

Returning to church following that retreat, my first action was to tear down the polished plaques. While packing them away, I heard in my inner ear the same refrain of

16

that hymn. Instead of feeling disappointed in removing the accolades, I sensed a prayerful relief realizing I was now better able to focus energies on worshiping and serving God. A bare wall and a prayer for humility brought me closer to God. Why hadn't I taken the plaques down sooner?

God of mercy, forgive our self-serving pride that separates us from you. Thank you for loving us even when we spend too much time loving ourselves. May your caring presence be the only treasure we need. Amen.

* *Words by Fred Pratt Green © Hope Publishing Co., Carol Stream, IL 60188. All rights reserved. Used by permission.*

MYRON R. CHARTIER

—⟨◦/◦/◦⟩—

Friends Matter

> David and Saul finished talking, and soon David and
> Jonathan became best friends. Jonathan thought as
> much of David as he did of himself. (1 Samuel 18:1, CEV)

Have you ever given thought to what friendship base you
will need in retirement? It's an important issue for those of
us approaching our senior years or already in them.
Friends are important to our social existence. As human
beings created in God's image, we are social creatures. As
people, we need people. That is God's design for us.

During our senior years we need a cadre of friends
who provide the kind of social support required for expe-
riencing our aging years. To experience the losses of our
senior years without the support of friends is to undergo
terrible isolation and loneliness.

A few years ago Jan and I attended a program named

AutumnQuest presented by the Midwest Career Development Service. This program for clergy planning for retirement helped us identify a place for retirement that would provide a friendship base for our aging years. As a result we will settle in southeast Denver and become a part of Calvary Baptist Church. We were members of this church when we were in graduate school at the University of Denver. Amazingly, many friends are still there and active. Many potential new friends are now a part of this church. We also have several friends in Colorado from our college years. A major reason for our choosing Colorado is because we believe our friendship support base will be in place and further nurtured.

People need people, especially as they age. The church community can be a great context for developing lifelong friends. In the church we have friends who share our faith in Jesus Christ, a common set of values, and a faith community.

We all need friends, as a passage in the Apocrypha highlights:

Faithful friends are a sturdy shelter;
whoever finds one has found a treasure.
Faithful friends are beyond price;

no amount can balance their worth.
Faithful friends are life-saving medicine;
and those who fear the Lord will find them.
Those who fear the Lord direct their friendship aright,
for as they are, so are their neighbors also.
(Sirach 6:14-17, NRSV)

Friends matter in our senior years.

Gracious God, our eternal friend, thank you for your friendship made possible through your sacrificial love expressed at the cross. Thank you for the friends we have, and guide us to new ones. Help us to be a loyal, faithful friend to others. Through Jesus, our friend and elder brother, we pray. Amen.

The Knowledge of God

If you indeed cry out for insight
   and raise your voice for understanding,
if you seek it like silver,
   and search for it as hidden treasures—
then you will understand the fear of the Lord
   and find the knowledge of God.
(Proverbs 2:3-5, NRSV)

How must I believe in a God I can neither see nor understand? That question has troubled many people who seek answers, for the question is difficult to solve.

More than forty years ago I saw a picture in a *Life* magazine I will never forget. It was a double-page collage of many scenes from the Bible. Beneath it were these words: "To him who believes, no explanation is necessary; to him who does not believe, no explanation is possible."

There are many things in this world today I do not understand. I can't understand how I can dial a few numbers and talk to my son ten thousand miles away in Okinawa. I can't understand why I am able to push a switch and fill my house with light. I do not understand how an airplane with hundreds of people on board can lift off the ground and fly six hundred miles an hour at thirty-five thousand feet up. And I certainly don't understand how my television and VCR work.

But I have faith that when I dial the numbers, my son will answer the phone. And that when I flick the switch, the lights will come on. Or that when I board the plane, the pilot will get me where I am going. Or that when I push the right buttons, I'll watch a movie or catch the news.

You see, I don't say, "I will never use electricity because I can't understand how it works," or "I will never call my children because I can't comprehend how the voices travel through the wires." We are always using things we don't understand, so why is it we say, "I can't believe God because I don't understand him"? We turn our backs on all the wonderful power God has placed at our disposal. Why? Lord, help our unbelief.

God of wisdom and mystery, how we make ourselves so small because we try to understand everything and act so foolish when we don't. We strive to comprehend your infinite nature with our finite minds. Rather than rejoicing in each new discovery as you reveal yourself to us in your perfect plan, we get angry because we want the whole pie and not just one bite at a time. Teach us again that understanding comes through an attitude of our hearts that places you in the center of what we hold most dear. In the name of him who is more precious than silver or gold. Amen.

ARTHUR J. CONSTIEN

———◦◦◦———

Graduation Promises

"Therefore everyone who hears these words of mine and puts them into practice is like a wise man who built his house on the rock." (Matthew 7:24, NIV)

"Come early so that we can get a seat," our son urged. A grandson was graduating from high school, and because inclement weather was expected, the exercises were moved from the football stadium to the gymnasium. Inside seating was limited, and since there were more than 950 graduates, latecomers would not find a seat.

Waiting for the ceremony to begin and to divert my attention from the discomfort of the bleachers, I calculated that this was the twenty-fifth graduation in my immediate family, including all levels, and there would be more to come in the approaching years.

Finally, the pomp and circumstance began. It took a good twenty minutes for all the graduates to reach their seats. Then came the usual greetings from the principal and the president of the class.

My aching back began to intensify my hope that there would be no long speeches, and, I must say, all the speeches were reasonable in length. The valedictorian and the salutatorian were probably well aware of the short attention span of their classmates.

The only other speech was by the chairman of the board of education, and he wasn't long, either. But I got to thinking about his situation. Being a graduation speaker may look like a golden opportunity to make a lasting impression on a large number of vulnerable people, and the temptation is strong to say more than one really needs to. But who will remember what is said? The speaker did try to impart some wisdom. But is a graduation the time and place? Besides, can the speaker guarantee that what he advises will produce what he promises?

When Jesus concluded his Sermon on the Mount, he told his hearers that if they heard what he was saying and put it into practice, they would be able to weather the storms of life. They would be like a wise person who builds a house on a solid foundation and not shifting sand, so that when the sudden torrents come roaring through, the house will survive.

Does Jesus guarantee his promise? He gave up his rightful place in the Godhead and became a human being, poor and suffering, for the right to say it. And he staked his life on what he said by willingly submitting to cruel crucifixion. That certainly says, "Trust me!"

For most graduation speakers I have to assume they are trustworthy. With Jesus, I know that he is; he showed it.

Lord, I hear what you are saying, and I am counting on it. Don't let me forget. Amen.

FRANK T. FAIR

———◦◦◦———

Put It in Your Head

Let this mind be in you which was also in Christ
Jesus. (Philippians 2:5, NKJV)

One day, nearly thirty years ago, when I picked up my
youngest son from preschool, he handed me a drawing
that he had made for me. Since the lines and colors had little resemblance to anything that I could identify, I tactful-
ly asked that he tell me what was in the picture. As he happily related the story with animals, trees, and airplanes as
major characters, I asked where were the bear, the birds,
the elephants, the trees, and the airplanes that he had mentioned. He started first to point out various markings as
different characters. Then he stopped and looked at me in
disgust and said, "Daddy, you have to put it in your head."

Four years ago I suffered a stroke that limited my ability to walk. As a result, I am partially confined to a wheel-

chair. One Sunday morning, as my wife struggled to get my chair from the trunk of the car and get me inside the church, we saw a cute little boy, who apparently lived in the neighborhood, standing there intensely eyeing every move we made. We spoke to him, and his returned hello was just above a whisper. In a flash he was gone. But before we finally got to the church's steps he came running back carrying several broken-off stems of wilted yellow dandelions that he held up to my wife and said, "Dese are for you." I was stunned and overwhelmed at such beauty of purpose as I saw my wife's eyes water as she bowed to give him a hug and thank him. At age four his head and his heart spoke volumes to us. But moreover, I no longer saw or smelled the odor of the dandelions. Instead there was transformed before my eyes a beautiful bouquet of golden, sun-kissed flowers sweetened by the purity and innocence of the little boy's smiling face that was couched in its center. It is that picture that is and will forever be etched in my head.

Sometime during our lifetime, if we live long enough, we will come in contact with unfamiliar markings or wilted dandelions, and the difference will be determined by our positive or negative attitude that we bring to the table of life. The things we put in our heads will determine the outcome. Is it not our personal responsibility to help make things better in this world? What if we decided in our heads that our weapons of judgment, blame, and criticism be made into plowshares of hope, love, and forgiveness to help cultivate the fertile fields of humanity? What if we put in our heads that wherever we are at this moment is the exact place we ought to be? What if we held the belief that all of our past mistakes were just lessons … lessons to help us fulfill our mission? And if we've learned our lessons well, then they will resonate in our determination to fulfill our purpose here on this earth. Then let us agree to put our heads to do what we must, for those we can, with what we have … right now.

Dear God, we praise and honor you for your mercy. We ask your help that we may put positive thoughts in our heads so that we may move closer to a global community of peace. Amen.

PATRICIA FARRELL

A New Beginning

The steadfast love of the Lord never ceases,
his mercies never come to an end;
they are new every morning;
great is your faithfulness.
"The Lord is my portion," says my soul,
"therefore I will hope in him."
(Lamentations 3:22-24, NRSV)

There are so many things I am planning to do now that I'm about to retire after fifty years of going to an office to work each day. The desire to be physically and mentally active is as strong in me as it was when I was fifteen years old and had my first job. But now my legs don't always want to hold me as I get out of bed each morning, and it takes a few minutes to get my body moving in a safe and secure way. My brain doesn't easily remember all the details as I go about my daily work. My hands don't move as quickly and surely as they used to do, and there is always a tension between what I want to do and can do. There isn't too much that I can count on in myself.

The words of the writer of Lamentations give me hope and comfort as I pray them now. I believe that the love and the strength of the Lord will remain steadfast as promised and that God's mercies will be granted as I do the seemingly small things each day. Such things as pushing my grandchild down the street and greeting the smiling faces of those who see us, painting the bedroom in my new apartment, or sitting quietly and reading a book. How much more I will need God to be with me now as I am aging. I need to listen to my soul and be reminded that God's mercies are new every morning—not just when I was young and the things I needed and wanted to do seemed so easy.

Dearest Creator God, you have given your sacred word that your love will never cease. I call on you each day to grant your mercies as I go about living fully the rest of my days here on earth and then with you eternally in heaven. Amen.

———❦———

An Unexpected Gift

> "Give, and it will be given to you. A good measure,
> pressed down, shaken together, running over, will be
> put into your lap; for the measure you give will be the
> measure you get back." (Luke 6:38, NRSV)

I was returning from work to my Minnesota farm home
when it happened. The engine of my Crosley clattered,
then froze tight. I depressed the clutch and rolled to a stop.
Now, how would I get to work tomorrow? Maybe I could
borrow my visiting grandparents' car. But they would be
returning to San Diego soon. They had even asked if I
could drive them home because Grandpa's eyes had got-
ten so bad. I had refused. I needed my job to be able to pay
my college fees.

I had a long walk ahead of me, so I set the brake and
stepped out onto the country road. That's when I saw the

tree. A lone tree grew close to the road. I had admired its perfect shape many times while driving by. But today the scene flashed into my mind with a sudden feeling of déjà vu. I'd had a dream several weeks before: the noise of the engine, the car coming to a stop, and that tree. I slumped back into the driver's seat and sat there in amazement. I had been shown these events in my dream before my grandparents made their request. What was I to do now? I knew the answer before the question formed in my mind. I would drive to San Diego. As I walked the four miles home there was excitement and a newfound joy in my heart. I knew I had made the right decision.

My grandfather had been an old-time missionary from his youth, traveling and preaching the gospel. Now in his late seventies, he needed help to complete this last journey, blessing the lives of those he had ministered to so many times before.

The drive west proved to be a turning point in my life. As we traveled from town to town and from home to home Grandpa told me wonderful stories of faith and inspiration. He talked of his hope for eternal life and of how God had blessed and helped him in his missionary work. There were stories of his youth on an Oklahoma farm and of his family's migration by wagon to Arizona. And when Grandpa slept Granny had stories of her own to tell.

I was able to return to college that fall, and I did earn a degree. But more important for me was the spiritual uplift and conviction that formed in my life and still encourages me after forty-seven years because I gave those precious weeks, that summer, to help my grandparents get home safely.

Thank you, God, for allowing me that precious time with my grandparents, so that I could learn of you through them. Help me to remember that time spent with your people is always an opportunity to learn of you. Amen.

MARJORIE HARRINGTON

━━∞∞∞━━

Bloom Where You Are Planted

And every day in the temple and at home they did not cease to teach and proclaim Jesus as the Messiah. (Acts 5:42, NRSV)

On my refrigerator door hangs a small magnet that tells me to "Bloom Where You Are Planted." I picked it up several years ago in the Crystal Cathedral gift shop on a visit to Garden Grove, California, and it has helped me many times to assess where I am at any given time in my walk with the Lord and what I am doing in that situation.

After the death of my pastor husband in 1996, I made the mistake of moving to a smaller apartment, where I spent the next three and a half years. I realized immediately that I had moved too soon and found that I didn't like

35

my new home because it was enclosed by tall cedars and buildings that kept the place dark and dreary.

However, I had a car and still drove, so I could get out most days. When an ice cream store opened for business not far from my apartment, I told my elderly neighbors, who had no available transportation, that I would take them to the store for a treat. Every few weeks thereafter, we went for hamburgers or chicken strips and the inevitable ice cream. We stopped at the grocery store or Wal-Mart for items they needed and generally ended up having a lot of fun together.

As much as my three friends enjoyed these excursions, I was the one who benefited the most. They helped to bring the sunshine back into my life.

When the apostles had been physically beaten by the council, they bloomed for God by teaching and preaching Jesus as the Christ just where they were, in the temple and in every house.

Dear Lord Jesus, help us, whatever our age or circumstances, to find our special niche in life. Some place where we can bring joy into the lives of others, who often need it so much. Amen.

—◦◦◦—

Whose Plans Are They Anyway?

For surely I know the plans I have for you, says the
Lord, plans for your welfare and not for harm, to give
you a future with hope. (Jeremiah 29:11, NRSV)

I remember how stimulated I would be after one of my
American literature classes. I'd rush in the house, pull off
my jacket, and head for the television room eager to share
my excitement with my husband.

But it was Monday night, and, as it does in many
American homes, Monday night meant football. In fact, I
had chosen Monday for my first college evening class
because it was my husband's bowling night. Growing up
in the 1950s, I knew it was okay for a wife to be away from
home when her husband also was out.

My attempts to share my newfound interest elicited a few grunts from Don. His eyes remained fixed on the screen's action. I'm not sure he even noticed as I slipped out of the room and retreated to the kitchen to fix a cup of tea. I wanted so badly to recapture the momentum of the lively discussion.

Soon the aroma of the tea and the warmth of the cup in my hands soothed my disappointment as I silently rehashed the poignant points raised during that evening's class. I didn't want to let go of the feelings of new life growing in me.

Those stirrings were the beginning of what became a time of profound change in my life. Looking back I see that this birthing process began years earlier with the discovery that a congenital malformation of my uterus made it impossible for me to carry a child to birth. My husband was not interested in adoption, and so my life's dream of being a mother died. Even more importantly, I lost my life's purpose.

It hadn't occurred to me to look beyond home and family for fulfillment. I wonder how many people's lives are not what they had in mind. I know mine isn't. I would never have chosen the pain of divorce or the loneliness of childlessness. Yet, after years of struggle and trying to understand God's plan for my life, I know that there is no pat answer. God has gifted me with life so that I may greet each day as an opportunity to create a blessing. I don't always succeed. But God is patient and good.

Creator God, help us to rely on you for everything. Take away our desire to figure out everything. We want to trust you. Forgive us when we look on others' lives with jealousy and envy. Make us content in simply being yours. Amen.

Margaret P. Bishop

———❦———

Model Behavior

Show yourself in all respects a model of good
works, and in your teaching show integrity, gravity.
(Titus 2:7, NRSV)

I'd like to tell you about my model for aging successfully;
she's not a Cheryl Tieggs or a Cindy Crawford, but a
Vivien Schaffner. Not famous, not renown, but wise and a
true role model for leading the way into the uncharted
waters of aging.

These are the lessons "Mrs. Schaffner," my model, is
teaching me.

1. Continue to invite new experiences. Stretch and grow.
Mrs. Schaffner, a ninety-year-old widow, might be tempt-
ed to rely on old information or experiences. Instead she's
interested in new ideas and challenges. On her ninetieth
birthday, she received a computer to use for e-mailing her

daughter and grandchildren. Although she is occasionally frustrated by the new technology (aren't we all?), nonetheless, she persists and is excited when she manages to reply to a message or send one of her own.

Recently Mrs. Schaffner moved into a two-bedroom apartment from her home of thirty years. "Oh, that must be very hard," people said to her. "Not really," she replied. She looked forward to redoing the apartment, getting new drapes and slipcovers, and making new friends.

2. Accept and accommodate changes that may occur with aging. When she was eighty-nine, Mrs. Schaffner had to forego her daily swim at the local community center, but now she uses weights instead. She no longer drives at night, but she toots around town during the day. She knows she can't do what she used to do, but these things she considers and allows for as she plans each day.

3. Balance reaching out to others with self-care. It's easy to get "out of whack"—to sit back in self-concern or to be so devoted to others that the self is lost. Mrs. Schaffner balances both priorities beautifully. She's director of a foreign-language bank, provides leadership in a local arts-and-crafts fair, is active in her church, often has lunch with friends, and participates in an ecumenical women's group, but she also takes time to nourish her spiritual life and to focus quietly on her thoughts.

4. Remain interested in others and their lives; be a listener. This is one of the most important lessons I've learned from my older friend. Although she is sad about the loss of many of her contemporaries, Mrs. Schaffner has cultivated new friendships by being interested in others. She enjoys vicariously the travels of others since she's no longer able to travel on her own.

Mrs. Schaffner admits to tiring of some older people's attention to the latest ache and pain. "It's so good to hear other kinds of talk," she says in discussing how she relishes current events and the ideas they generate.

Mrs. Schaffner is remarkable; she's optimistic, capable of warm love, and open to new adventures and challenges. As I age, I want to emulate her positive approach—her interest in life in tandem with acceptance of the changes that aging brings. I'm happy to call her my friend and my "true" model. Perhaps we all can learn lessons from her.

God, we give thanks that you provide models to show us how to live fully and faithfully. In Christ's name, the one who is the greatest model of all. Amen.

PATRICIA A. KOHLS

———✿✿✿———

Discovering Harmony

Live in harmony with one another. (Romans 12:16, NRSV)

Preparing for our spring concert took many hours of rehearsals for both our orchestra and the choir. First the vocal sections needed sopranos, altos, and baritones to blend all their words and notes into a melody of perfect harmony. All of the instruments in the orchestra needed to be in supportive harmony. The orchestra conductor and individual musicians interacted at every note to bring about their presence in musical unity. The reality was that it took lots of effort from each person to reach our goal of producing beautiful music for the concert. One or more people out of sync could put the symphony out of tune. Each person had to focus on his or her thoughts and actions with a powerful awareness to stay in tune. Every musician had to stay alert to the conductor and his movements.

God is the conductor in our lives, and we need to focus on the divine presence to stay in tune. God directs and draws us together, blessing each of us with his love, and bringing our relationships into an understanding harmony.

God can give us the encouragement and strength to overcome and let go of past negative experiences that might put us out of sync, causing us to be out of tune with our life's harmony. Abiding in his will and strength we can once again discover harmony each day.

Our thoughts and words create an action that brings an echoing effect and touches us like a melody reverberating. Our friendships bless and resound lightly in tune to God's constant and endless flowing love for each of us.

While we are orchestrating a project we can be responsible and accountable with thoughtful actions toward a focused purpose in our symphony of life. Being a good communicator, alert to our listening and speaking kind words, can help us discover a warm, supportive harmony in our community.

Thank you, Creator Lord, for all the gifts you have given me. Grant me alertness to always live in understanding harmony with those around me. Amen.

—————

Giving, the Eternal Way

"For where your treasure is, there your heart will be also." (Matthew 6:21, NRSV)

In *Who Switched the Price Tags?* Tony Campolo tells of a study in which fifty people over ninety-five years old answered the question "If you could live your life over again, what would you do differently?"

One answer that was given over and over was "I would do more things that would live on after I die."

As I examine my own life, I see much of my time, money, and energy is spent in getting through another day of cleaning, talking to family and friends, shopping for groceries, washing clothes and dishes. Very little of my life today will live on after I die. How can I change that?

I am rich in the things of this world. We live in Florida in the winter months, in Maine during the summers. We eat in restaurants often and enjoy good food, good water, good television. Most of the people in the world cannot do or have these things. But how in the world is my wealth living on after I die? The money we give to the church and charities may, but is that all we can do? We read over and over the story of the widow's mite. We know we are to give, but empty our billfolds? Lord!

We can give and give and give again. We can give ourselves to the future by teaching a Sunday school class or befriending neighborhood children and youth in our church. (Do we even know their names?) Living on in the memory of family members and those we have befriended is a powerful memorial. If we have the material resources, we can give scholarships to those going on to vocational school or college (even a small amount helps and encourages), or give to endowment funds that keep producing interest long after we are gone.

All of us have so much to give. We may all find more ways to use what we have for God.

Precious Lord, help me remember my treasure is in you. May I share all I have, all I am with others. I praise you and thank you for calling me yours. Amen.

—◦◦◦—

Return to Trust

"Can any of you by worrying add a single hour to your span of life? If then you are not able to do so small a thing as that, why do you worry about the rest?" (Luke 12:25-26, NRSV)

When I was a child I was afraid of the dark. One night when I was particularly nervous, I asked God to watch over me. Immediately I was overcome by a deep sense of peace. I knew at a very deep level that God was there and would protect me.

That assurance surrounded me for years. I was not afraid of anything, because I knew who was in charge. I walked home alone at night. I enjoyed thunderstorms, hurricanes, and blizzards. I took risks of leadership and attempted many things that in my own strength I would have not thought myself able to do.

I don't remember when it was, but sometime in adulthood, my awareness of God's constant presence faded from my mind. Little things would worry me. The more I relied on myself—on my ability to meet whatever challenge faced me—the more anxiety became a daily traveling companion.

I am now well past the age of fifty. The goal for the second half of my life is to return to the trust and faith of my youth. The older I get the more difficult my daily work becomes. The sooner I realize that alone I am not up to the task, the sooner I will put my trust in God, knowing that God is able to do what I could never do alone. Each and every day that I ask God to guide my path and show me the way is a day free from fear and anxiety.

God who sees and knows my every need, today I put my trust and faith in you, knowing that you alone are sufficient. Amen.

—ɔʘɔ—

Brighten the Corner

"You are the light of the world." (Matthew 5:14, NRSV)

"Brighten the Corner Where You Are" is a song that comes to many of us out of our childhood Sunday school days. Its basic message to us is to let our light shine wherever we are, even in the commonplace, humdrum, everyday events of our lives.

As a minister, I always hope and pray that the Sunday sermon will be a bright light, touching many people with a message that will be remembered throughout life. The reality is, however, that while the sermon is important in teaching God's Word and inspiring the congregation to follow Christ, it is rarely so brilliant that it is remembered for more than a few days.

This truth became evident when my wife and I celebrated our fiftieth wedding anniversary. Friends from the churches we had pastored sent letters of congratulations and related memories they recalled from our ministry with them. Only one mentioned a particular sermon that was etched indelibly on her mind. More often, many people recalled incidents that let God's light shine through a very human pastor.

One lady, not a member of the church, wrote of the time her husband (who was a member) was sick and I had come to call on him. She met me at the door, flustered, upset, and angry. Her washing machine had broken, and water and soapsuds covered the floor. Her memory was that I asked for a mop, cleaned up the mess, and then visited with her husband. For her, that was a brightened corner—even a little of the light of the world.

One brief letter summed up the impact of a Christian's light upon another life: "One never forgets the pastor who took your hand when you asked Jesus into your heart. Also, one never forgets the pastor who baptized you—or at [a child's] young age of twelve, helped you to bury your father. Thank you for my memories of you. Phyllis."

There's a sequel to this letter. I wrote a note of appreciation to Phyllis, and a few weeks later I received a reply from her husband. He wrote that his wife received my letter and read it just before she died after a long struggle with cancer.

Never think of your life as insignificant, for the light that comes to you through faith in the Savior can brighten the corner of other lives for time and eternity.

Eternal God, thank you for entrusting to us your light so that others may come to know you. Help us to brighten the corner of another life today. Amen.

Wanda Naylor

———— ✺✺✺ ————

Make a Joyful Noise

Make a joyful noise to the LORD, all the earth....
For the LORD is good;
his steadfast love endures forever,
and his faithfulness to all generations.
(Psalm 100:1,5, NRSV)

As a small child sitting in church with my grandfather listening to the organist playing, I would put my hands on my lap and pretend that I was playing with her. I said to myself, "Someday I want to be the organist of my church."

But then came the Depression. There was no money for lessons. I had to quit school and start working to help my family. In my own power, there was no way I would ever become the organist I dreamed of becoming. But God knew the deepest desire of my heart. It took more than twenty years, but God opened many doors that eventually led to my being the organist of my church.

I played in my church for thirty years, and today I still play at the retirement community where I live.

Do you have a deep desire to do some good in this world? Do you have a God-given talent that needs to be exercised? Ask God to show you the way, for with God all things are possible.

God, giver of all gifts, show us how to dedicate our best selves to your service, today and every day. May we always use them to honor and glorify your name. Amen.

—◦∕◦∕◦—

The Rearview Mirror

I am your God;
I will strengthen you, I will help you,
I will uphold you with my victorious right hand.
(Isaiah 41:10, NRSV)

God called me to missionary service during my teen years. During the subsequent years of preparation, I married and began my family. In 1950 we were appointed to Japan, where we began our missionary service, feeling completely in God's will.

Much to our sorrow, our service was terminated by the death of my husband. With a young family, I found it necessary to remain in the States. I agonized over this, unable to reconcile myself to the reality of the situation in light of my missionary call. How could God call me and then not make a way for me to continue in that service?

I later married another minister. His work took us to several parishes and theological schools around the country. Each time we moved, I carved out a place for myself. First I taught school. Then I became a workshop leader and led seminars in the Midwest. I continued to seek God's will in each situation, but the jobs seemed to have little connection with each other, leading nowhere.

Finally, following ordination to the ministry, I took a position as church relations director of an American Baptist-related college, seeking better financial support from the churches for the college. I enjoyed each of the positions, but how could I give up the missionary call that was so clear to me?

One day I learned that international ministries sought to fill the position of area director for southern Asia. Studying the profile, I learned that ordination was a plus. Organizational skills were necessary, something I had learned as chair of a large high school English department. Familiarity with budgets was required, a skill I had developed as church relations director. Confidence in public speaking, such as I had learned through the leading of retreats, was important. Finally, the candidate should have served somewhere in Asia as a missionary!

I applied and was given that position, and after two years I was made director of the overseas division, with the responsibility for overseeing mission work throughout the world where American Baptists had missionaries. I soon realized that though I couldn't always see God's hand along the way, God was surely guiding me throughout the years as my life came full circle back to missionary service. Yes, sometimes we see God's guidance through the rearview mirror of our lives, as we look back on our path.

Dear God, help us to walk by faith and not by sight, trusting you at every step. Amen.

——⟨∞∞⟩——

Making Decisions

And what does the Lord require of you
but to do justice, and to love kindness,
and to walk humbly with your God?
(Micah 6:8, NRSV)

As I think back over the years of my life, I often wonder if all of my decisions were good ones. Once I was expressing this to one of our daughters. She said to me, "Mother, if you hadn't done that you wouldn't have been you."

My years as a pastor's wife were lived in an era of specific expectations. I was to be a helpmate to my husband, have well-behaved children, keep a clean and neat house, teach Sunday school classes, be active in churchwomen's work. All of these things I tried to do.

But there came the time when I wrote a letter to the editor of the local newspaper expressing my view on a controversial issue. That didn't go over very well. Later I ran for a seat on the local school board. A Lutheran pastor had resigned from the board. He had been well received by the community, and I felt a Baptist pastor's wife would do well on the board. I won the board seat and thought all was well, only to learn that I was really in hot water. I had stepped outside the circle of correctness for a pastor's wife. I proposed some curriculum changes that were considered to be suspect. When people didn't understand something, the easiest term to use was "Communist."

One night the phone rang. When I answered it, the voice at the other end said, "How would you like to have your tongue cut out of your mouth?" The caller hung up. I slumped to the chair unable to speak. When I was finally able to tell my husband what had happened, he called the police. Soon a policeman and a detective were in our home. We explained the call, as well as the fact that my husband was leaving the next morning for a three-week seminar. I would be alone at the parsonage with our two children, high school and junior high ages. The police assured us that they would patrol the house each night.

No harm came to us, but it is an experience our children, now adults, and I will never forget. There were many times I said to myself, "If I had just kept quiet, this would not have happened." I have learned, though, that our Christian faith and popularity do not always go hand in hand.

In our lifetime we saw the Iran-Contra conflict divide families, friends, and churches. We were proud of our youngest daughter when she made two trips with Witness for Peace to Nicaragua. This was the daughter who could remember the night her mother received the threat of having her tongue cut out. It didn't keep her from taking controversial positions.

Holy God, you have given us the ability to make decisions. Guide us in all ways to make wise ones, to do justice, to love kindness, and to walk humbly with you. Amen.

John H. Pipe

——⟡⟡⟡——

When Forgiving Just Once Is a Big Step

"Again, truly I tell you, if two of you agree on earth about anything you ask, it will be done for you by my Father in heaven. For where two or three are gathered in my name, I am there among them."

Then Peter came and said to him, "Lord, if another member of the church sins against me, how often should I forgive? As many as seven times?" Jesus said to him, "Not seven times, but, I tell you, seventy-seven times." (Matthew 18:19-22, NRSV)

"We need to pray for the families of the two boys who killed and injured so many at Columbine." Kathy Ireland, the mother of Patrick Ireland, shared this prayer request during a chapel service at Craig Hospital. Patrick was one of the twenty-six students injured in the shooting spree in Littleton, Colorado, on April 20, 1999. He and three other students went through an extensive rehabilitation program at Craig Hospital in Colorado. Patrick has a traumatic brain injury caused by bullets in his head.

As a volunteer chaplain at Craig, I was leading worship three weeks after the shooting and asked for prayer requests. Patrick and his mother were there. Also present were four other patients and family members and a dozen of Patrick's friends and families from the high school and his church, Columbine United Church in Littleton.

As Mrs. Ireland shared her concern, I wondered if I could pray for anyone who might threaten, let alone maim or kill, my children or grandchildren. Would I be able to forgive? I thought of the times I tried to forgive someone for what he or she had done to me. Had I forgiven? Was I holding onto resentments? My experiences fell far short of the horror that Patrick, his school pals, and his family have been going through.

These young people will be physically and emotionally scarred for life. Doctors estimate that they were struck by as many as twenty-four bullets, and many of those bullets will remain in their bodies as a reminder of the carnage through which they lived. In my attempts to minister to these patients and families at Craig, I have been amazed at their resiliency and will to move on. Their families and churches are surrounding these young patients, and their families, with support, encouragement, faith, hope, and love. What an amazing witness to the power of the gospel in the midst of tragedy.

Healing God, I am grateful for the witness of those who have suffered outrageous hurts and are able to heal, forgive, and be a witness to the love of Christ. Amen.

Dolores Grandfield Rodgers

———◦◦◦———

On the Way

"Were not our hearts burning within us while he was talking to us on the road, while he was opening the scriptures to us?" (Luke 24:32, NRSV)

At age sixty-four, I have reached what society refers to as my Golden Years. I had some golden years as a wife, then as a widow and single parent, but I was always impatient and always in a hurry then. As I reflect on my life, I realize that a good deal of my time was spent in perpetual motion without ever giving much thought to the journey.

Insecurity and fear of the unknown eventually turned me into an emotional and physical wreck. My spiritual life consisted of attendance at Sunday liturgy, occasionally at daily Mass, and an annual three-day spiritual retreat. My personal prayer life involved petitioning God to help me with what I thought I wanted, not what I needed.

Little did I know that my spiritual life was about to undergo major reconstruction.

Then one momentous day a friend invited me to attend a prayer meeting.

"What's a prayer meeting?" I asked.

"Come and see," she responded. So I went and kept on going every Tuesday evening. The people in that group had something I wanted and needed. Before that time, I had known about Jesus, but afterward, I truly knew Jesus as my personal Savior. I was empowered to live life with renewed strength and complete trust in God. My philosophy now is to live each day as if it were my last because in reality, it may very well be!

The people I encounter on the way are no longer strangers, but rather sisters and brothers in the body of Christ. The disciples who encountered Christ on the road to Emmaus did not recognize Jesus at first, but they came to know him—along the way.

Giver of life, let us recognize you in our sisters and brothers as we journey this road together.

—◦◦◦—

Love Letters

Pleasant words are a honeycomb,
sweet to the soul and healing to the bones.
(Proverbs 16:24, NIV)

Two of my favorite letters were written about fifty years apart. The first, from my father, I received at camp when I was a preteen. I was in that know-it-all stage and often corrected my dad's grammar. Dad was an accomplished cabinetmaker with only a fifth-grade education. In his letter he left out all the punctuation as he told about events that were happening at home. It ended with "Love Your Dad P S Here are all the marks I left out .??;;—,,,!!!" How I giggled as I showed the letter to my friends.

The second letter I received last Mother's Day from my oldest son. In it he recalls some of the things he learned growing up in our home. Steve, a parent himself now and a senior manager in a computer consulting firm, closes with the following words: "So many simple life-lessons are flooding back, such as 'Don't wear stripes with plaids' or 'Always look both ways.' I especially appreciate the grammar lessons that help me communicate effectively now, though I didn't like them at the time. Thank you for all you have given me, and the grace with which you gave it. Peace and delight on this, your special day." What warmth for this mother's heart.

While my father was alive I said far too few encouraging and uplifting things to him. I could have thanked him for all the beautiful things he made for me out of wood, for his love and support of the family, and for the way he modeled the Christian walk. I could have remembered all the toys he repaired, the games he made for us, and the puzzles and tricks he so enjoyed. How much better to find something positive to say rather than finding fault.

I'm glad Steve remembers some happy and good learning. I'm also glad he was willing to share that with me.

God of us all, young and old, grant us tolerance and kindness and love for all those with whom we share your world. Amen.

—⟨ɷɷ⟩—

An Emergency Broadcast System

I can do all things through Christ who strengthens me.
(Philippians 4:13, NKJV)

"This is a test of the emergency broadcast system. In the event of an actual emergency, you would be asked to tune to … " How many times has my favorite radio or television show been interrupted with that announcement? And it doesn't matter how many times I've heard it; it still bothers my routine. While it reminds me to be prepared for bad weather that may come, I'd rather not be reminded. I have to admit I don't have any batteries in my radio. I look out the window during the announcement, and it is a beautiful, sunny day. By the time the announcement is over I've already tuned it out. I know this is only a test.

I'll be prepared when the true emergency comes.

It's amazing how I can lull myself into false complacency when things are going well. I don't need God's help. I have even been known to take the credit!

My storms are big decisions and painful experiences. There have been times when what I faced was insurmountable from my vantage point. Many times I didn't have the right equipment—all the information I needed to make decisions. My thinking was clouded with uncertainty, anger, and fear. I fell back into the old pattern that all things can be handled by me.

I have used my emergency system. I know it works. When painful decisions or disaster come into my life, I know to focus on God. God, not I, has the solutions. And he's ready to reveal it to me if I am prepared to listen. By daily prayer and meditations, I can tune in. I may falter, friends may disappoint me, and family may be gone, but with his strength, I am ready to face life.

God, may I never be complacent about your presence in my life. Troubles may come and go, but you give me the strength to face it all. Today I acknowledge my weakness and claim your strength. Amen.

Too Many Gifts, Too Little Love

> He looked up and saw rich people putting their gifts into the treasury; he also saw a poor woman put in two small copper coins. He said, "Truly I tell you, this poor widow has put in more than all of them; for all of them have contributed out of their abundance, but she out of her poverty has put in all she had to live on." (Luke 21:1-4, NRSV)

One day as I was walking through a department store, I overheard a woman say, "If that happened to me, I would really be upset. Imagine going to a friend's garage sale and finding the gift you gave her on a table still in its box. No wonder she was insulted." That unfortunate incident had strained the relationship between the giver and the receiver and offended others as well. To express love and kindness, gifts must be appropriate, or they may place the receiver in a difficult position. How do you thank someone who gives you flowers that trigger your allergies, or a punch bowl and cups that you have no room for in your house? No matter how good our intentions are, we are bound to make mistakes from time to time.

Several years ago my husband and I visited his elderly aunt in Mississippi. Her once lovely home showed signs of neglect. She no longer had the energy or the strength to care for it. As I sat in her living room, my eyes were drawn to an ornately crafted but tarnished silver gravy boat in her china cabinet. It was obviously very difficult to polish.

Just as that thought crossed my mind, Aunt Pearl said, "Beverly, you like that, don't you? My neighbor gave it to me last Christmas with the sugar bowl and creamer to match. Pretty, aren't they?" "Yes, very pretty," I replied, but I wondered silently why anyone would give such gifts to a woman in her eighties who was clearly unable to entertain dinner guests. "I've never used them," she said. "I want you and Allen to have them." I protested, but Aunt Pearl felt burdened by those gifts, and we carried them home.

I polished those silver pieces and put them away until

my sister-in-law came to visit. She remembered them and politely admired them. I explained that they didn't look appropriate with my less formal tableware and offered them to her. She accepted them graciously. Six years later she admitted to me that she didn't want them either.

I've often wondered why we feel obliged to give so many gifts. I've kept gifts for years that I would never have chosen for myself. Even though we are willing to live with heavy debt to meet perceived expectations, the gifts we buy often fall short when it comes to making the receiver feel loved or cared for. A house full of toys cannot satisfy children who receive too little attention from their parents, and a huge basket of fruit or ornate silver serving pieces will not make an elderly person feel less lonely. Appropriate gifts are those that meet a need. A listening ear, a shared experience, or a helping hand are what most people need and want. They come wrapped in lovely memories.

God of all good gifts, help us to discern one another's needs and to give appropriately.

ANN S. KRAMER

———◦◦◦———

A Painful Love

For God so loved the world that he gave his only Son,
so that everyone who believes in him may not perish
but may have eternal life. (John 3:16, NRSV)

Through my Christian walk, I think the most awesome
and wonderful revelation has been the gradual understanding of the nature of God's love for us. There is no way
to completely comprehend this love here on earth. It is too
vast and perfect.

But there have been times when I have been given
glimpses of it. One of those times was shortly after our
unmarried daughter announced that she was pregnant.
My husband and I reached out to her in love, but oh, that
love was so full of pain and longing! We continued to pray
and ask God to help us all through this difficult situation.
I began to see that if I loved my child so totally in her

predicament, how much more does our heavenly Father love us. And his love for us is also full of pain and longing when he sees us so often going astray. In fact he loved us so much that he sent his only Son to die for us.

O Father, till today
I've never really known your love.
The aching, longing pain,
The agony contained,
Until I knew that love myself
For my own child.
My fleshly mother's love pierced through.
O Father, I'm just starting to know you.

You seek your child,
Your heart breaks like my own
When your precious little one has lost the way
And weak and floundering
Is blown and tossed today.

O Father,
till this hour
I've never praised you from

A heart that knows
Your love is full of pain and longing.
That you chose to bear this pain for me,
For all the lost ones brought to thee,
O Father, I will thank you for that love eternally.

Lord God, thank you for your everlasting love, the love that caused you to send Jesus to die on our behalf. Help us to have ever-increasing love for your children here on earth. Amen.

————— ∞ —————

God Makes It Possible

"For mortals it is impossible, but for God all things are possible." (Matthew 19:26, nrsv)

One of the saddest things I frequently hear people say is "Oh, I can't do that"—I can't sing. Or I can't fly. Or I can't drive in the city. Or I can't pray aloud. Or I can't—you name it.

Once we say "I can't!" it becomes true. As long as we think we can't, we never will.

Jesus said, "For mortals it is impossible, but for God all things are possible."

I have seen people do incredible things once they believe that with God's help they are able. One of the women in my Sunday school class, who was paralyzed, is now learning to use a computer so that she will be able to work again. Work again? When paralyzed from the neck down? With God's help she will be able.

When I accepted my first job in ministry, one of the requirements was to edit a newsletter. This was very scary to me. I had never done such a thing. I did not feel I was up to the task. One of my colleagues told me just to start, and if I ever got stuck she would help me. What seemed like one big impossible task, I soon learned, was many little tasks that needed to be done one after the other.

In the fourteen years I have worked in ministry, I have edited not only a newsletter but also many articles, journals, and even two books. What seems impossible to us can be done if we will let God show us the way.

God of all possibilities, today help me to resist the urge to say "I can't" and instead to say "With your help I am able." Amen.

RUTH H. MARSTALLER

—◦◦◦—

Cleaning Up the Debris

"I am the vine, you are the branches. Those who abide in me and I in them bear much fruit, because apart from me you can do nothing." (John 15:5, NRSV)

Maine suffered a terrible ice storm in January 1998. Whenever a door or window was opened, tree branches could be heard cracking, breaking, and falling. Trees and electric poles entangled with wires covered the roads.

More than two years later a once beautifully landscaped home near our Baptist Conference Center is still surrounded by fourteen broken and dead birch trees. No dead growth has been removed; no new trees have been planted. The house and grounds look eerie and grotesque—a good setting for a Dracula movie.

What a shame. But even more tragic are the dead and broken branches in my life. I know God will prune these branches as I abide in Christ. Yet I hold fast to my resentments against others and regrets as I relive my mistakes and failures. I cling to my bad habits because they are so comfortable, and besides, no one's perfect.

Often I find myself wondering why others continue to do wrong. Do they know they are hurting others when they speak so sharply to them? Do they realize how greedy they are when they complain about the causes that keep asking for help? Do they know it's wrong to cheat even when they aren't caught? Are they aware they are setting a bad example when they smoke or drive while intoxicated? Do they know they need a little pruning here and there?

And then I bow my head and ask God to be merciful to me, a sinner. And I know I am the one who needs the pruning, who needs God's help in all I do and say and think.

Dear Lord, help me to abide in you, to focus on you and not look at others. I need your divine healing as I seek to be whole and well, able to serve you with all that I am, all that I have. Amen.

DOLORES GRANDFIELD RODGERS

—<small>❧❧❧</small>—

Varieties of Gifts

Now there are varieties of gifts, but the same Spirit;
and there are varieties of services, but the same
Lord; and there are varieties of activities, but it is
the same God who activates all of them in everyone.
(1 Corinthians 12:4-5, NRSV)

I grew up in a large city on the East Coast, the second of
four children whose parents were hard-working individuals who instilled religious values in their children. I always
knew that I wanted to serve God in a special way, but felt
unworthy. While a fifty-two-year-old student at Cabrini
College in Radnor, Pennsylvania, I volunteered to serve in
New York City for four months in a ministry that reached
out to the frail elderly who lived alone. I felt fulfilled by this
work and considered myself a missionary of sorts.

After college, my regular employment was far more

mundane and less satisfying. However, my childhood dreams of being a missionary seemed to come true when, at age sixty-three, I was one of nineteen elders who embarked on a spiritual journey serving in various ministries as members of the Jesuit Elder Corps in the Pacific Northwest.

I have been told by my family and friends that my decision to join this Catholic Volunteer Corps took a great deal of courage and faith. To me, it was simply the answer to prayer. That one year of ministry in Seattle was quite an opportunity and challenge especially for someone who had spent her entire life on the East Coast. I placed my trust in God and although there were disappointments—personality clashes in our six-person community, two months spent back East for major surgery, a long commute to the site where I served—I reminded myself each day that God had given me a gift to be cherished, the gift of service.

When I returned home, I felt vaguely dissatisfied. What would my next challenge be? Where would I find another opportunity to serve God as I had in Seattle? It was during one of my prayer times that it came to me that I had been serving God by performing ordinary tasks day by day.

As a child, I thought that in order to be a disciple, it was necessary to give up all my possessions and follow in Jesus' footsteps. Not so. We serve every day in the small tasks we do for those around us. At home in New Jersey I have begun transporting an elder to church and to her other appointments. Recently I visited a friend in Minnesota, washed her windows, and cooked meals for her and her invalid mother. I know now that the gift of service can be used anywhere—in Washington state, in Minnesota, or in New Jersey—and to serve strangers or family members.

All-seeing God, help us to see and respect the small acts of service and kindness we do for others as part of our love for you.

Insights into Revelation

CAROL SPARGO PIERSKALLA

The Hedgerow

A PARABLE

During our lifetime, we acquire quite a few bruises, scars, bad habits, and even some neuroses. Character traits that may have been useful to us once for survival are now impediments to our spiritual journey. As we age, we hold on to memories of hurts, even those that occurred in childhood, and the accumulation of such memories can be crippling.

A few years ago, when I was dealing with some of my own old bruises, I had a vision of myself as a farmer hiding my "garbage" behind a hedgerow and being too ashamed to ask for help when the trash became a noxious blight. I may have hidden it from my neighbors, but it still poisoned my life. Examining those old bruises and neuroses, especially in the healing illumination of God's revelation—in Scripture and in Creation—was the beginning of freedom for me. May it be so for you as well.

Some years ago in a land many of us have visited, there lived a farmer who owned a beautiful piece of land. He had inherited the land from his parents, who had inherited it from their parents. They had cultivated the land well and were known throughout the community for its beautiful fields and quality produce. The farmer took great pride in his land and was very gratified when his neighbors complimented him or asked his advice on their own crops.

However, there was one small area of his farm that displeased him. It is true that it wasn't very noticeable because it was at the far end of his land, but being a perfectionist, he worried about it. This was an area that had been used for generations as the family dump. After all, farmers had old machinery, scraps of corn stalks, rocks, kitchen scraps, old clocks that didn't work any longer, even the occasional stunted or imperfect crop that had to be tossed out. After several hundred years of dumping, this area had become an eyesore.

Being a practical man as well as a proud one, the farmer

decided to plant a beautiful hedgerow of trees enclosing this area and shielding it from the view of his neighbors and himself. He chose fast growing and very dense evergreens. In no time he could look from his porch and see a green curtain, summer and winter, instead of the mounds of unpleasant refuse. More importantly, none of his neighbors could see it either, and soon his neighbors forgot it was there. The farmer himself forgot about it most of the time.

Then, one summer as he was walking through his fields, the farmer came upon a patch of stunted corn. He could find no blight, no insect or pest; the corn was simply not growing properly. He pulled the corn up angrily, then returned to his chores and forgot about it. But over the next few weeks he came upon potatoes that had rotted in the ground, soybean plants with empty pods, and more stalks of stunted corn.

"Well, no matter," he said. "Next spring when I plant over again, this will probably just disappear."

But the next year, the ruined crops were even more common. "No matter," thought the farmer. "Most of my land is good and productive. A few bad spots don't really matter. After all, this land is old and can't be expected to produce perfectly forever."

And so he went on about his business, ignoring the occasional imperfect crops and unproductive areas of land. Mostly he was bothered that his neighbors might see them. So he transplanted seedlings from his original evergreen hedgerow to shield these new areas from view as well.

One day as the farmer was taking a fairly repulsive load of junk to the dump, instead of refusing to see what was there, he took a quick look around. He'd been hearing a great deal about recycling, and he realized that some of this accumulation might be recyclable. Some might actually be valuable as antiques. While he was standing there wondering how in the world to begin such a big job, his neighbor came by. The farmer was overcome with shame. To think that anyone should see such a mess!

"If you're thinking of having a go at cleaning this up," the neighbor said, "I might be able to help. I had an even worse mess on my property, and last year I cleaned it up with the help of one of my friends. I'd be glad to help."

"Well…." The farmer hesitated. Imagine the shame of having someone see all the stuff that was dumped here!

He felt a hand on his shoulder. "Come on," said his neighbor. "It's much easier if we do it together."

It was a miserable job. They had to find someplace that

recycled; they had to find antique shops that valued his family's accumulation from generations back. Then they had to sort out the material that the farmer could use for his own life. Some of what was left had to be taken to the huge landfill nearby. Too, some material could be used as compost and plowed under.

Finally, the sorting and discarding complete, the farmer planted a new crop behind the hedgerow. Then he waited.

The community was very surprised to see the farmer out in his field in the spring, cutting down the hedgerow that had stood for years at the back of his property.

"What are you doing?" his neighbors exclaimed. "That was a very nice hedgerow."

"But I don't need it any more," explained the farmer. "It was to shield my dumping area from my sight and yours. But look what is behind it now!"

The neighbors gazed in astonishment at row upon row of tulips of every color imaginable.

"I planted them last fall," explained the farmer with pride. "I wasn't sure what would happen in this abused soil, but the tulips seem to be thriving."

Over the next few years, all the hedgerows on the

farmer's property were taken down. The chemicals and poisons that had leeched from the dumping area into his fields were no longer there to cause the blight. When the tulips finished blooming, the farmer planted salvia and marigolds, impatiens and begonias, hollyhocks and gladioli.

And each evening in the spring and early summer, the farmer sat on his porch (sometimes with his neighbor) looking out over his fields at row after row of tulips and marveled at the ability of the land to recover and bloom in spite of the abuse it suffered.

The Scriptures Came Alive

"Were not our hearts burning inside us as he spoke to us on the road and opened the Scriptures to us?" (Luke 24:32, NAB)

In the years when I taught a religion class, the Bible for me, represented the history of our Christian faith. But eight years ago I found that God would use the Scriptures to teach me about his incredible love.

Late one evening in 1991, I lay awake in my bedroom staring into the dark. The sudden, tragic death of my older sister consumed my thoughts. My mind, filled with grief, could not find rest. I slipped out of bed, took my Bible, and went downstairs. I longed to find some relief from my despair in the pages of the ancient book.

I sat on the davenport in the front room and flipped open the Scriptures. To my surprise, a passage leaped from the page. John 14:27 (TLB) said, "I am leaving you with a gift—peace of mind and heart! And the peace I give isn't fragile like the peace the world gives. So don't be troubled or afraid." This idea startled me. Jesus was telling me he wanted to give me a gift, and if I received it I would find an inner peace in all the turmoil.

Confused, I wasn't ready to accept what Jesus offered. But I believed Jesus wanted me to have the peace only he could give. I wrote the date 10/13/91 down next to the passage; I knew that one day I would want to remember the first night the Scriptures came alive.

After that I read the Bible daily. I couldn't get enough of what Jesus had to say to me in the Scriptures. His words told me how important I am to him and why he came to suffer, die, and rise. Jesus has taken me on an amazing journey, healing my broken heart and teaching me to let go and allow him to enter into my life.

At a Bridal Love Retreat, in June 1996, while rereading the passage of John 14:27, I realized the peace Jesus had offered me so long ago was now mine.

Lord Jesus, we thank you for making the Scriptures alive and vibrant. Amen.

—◦/◦/◦—

Beatitudes for the Service Employee

"Blessed are the poor in spirit … those who mourn … the meek … those who hunger and thirst for righteousness … the merciful … the pure in heart … the peacemakers … those who are persecuted for righteousness' sake … you when people revile you and persecute you and utter all kinds of evil against you falsely on my account." (Matthew 5:3-11, NRSV)

I was approaching retirement from my company after thirty-three years of service. What could I say at my retirement party to encourage my colleagues? Had I learned anything from all those years of helping someone else solve problems? Technical service employees rarely became company heroes and, in fact, counted themselves lucky if a client even took time to say thanks.

Listening one Sunday to a sermon on the Beatitudes, I realized that Jesus could have been speaking directly to just such folks. In contemporary America he might have said it something like this:

*Blessed are the poorly paid, for they will not be
    corrupted by excessive wealth or possessions.*
*Blessed are those who mourn for by-passed promotions,
    for they shall be comforted by the majority.*
*Blessed are the meek, for they are certain to inherit at
    least average merit increases, little hassle from
    management or co-workers, and a low risk of
    termination during restructuring.*
*Blessed are those who hunger and thirst for what is
    right and true, for they shall know deep satisfaction
    and peace from their honesty.*
*Blessed are the merciful, for they shall generate lasting
    friendships with both clients and colleagues.*
*Blessed are the pure in heart, for they shall reap the
    rewards of a fine reputation for trustworthiness.*
*Blessed are the peacemakers, for they shall become one
    of the community of unsung heroes.*

Blessed are you when others revile you and persecute you and utter all kinds of evil against you falsely because you have done what is right and true, for you will sleep soundly each night without guilt. Rejoice and be glad, for your reward is great in heaven, for so men persecuted the prophets who were before you.

An illuminating career question on employee surveys asks, How often do you go home after work with a feeling of satisfaction? I learned that a truly happy service employee must generate deep internal satisfaction from the act of helping others. It has to come from within, not from rewards.

Lord God, as I trudge off to work this morning, help me remember your Son's list of character traits. It's doubtful anyone will say thanks today, and that's okay. Amen.

BERNICE HILL BORZEKA

———❦———

Consider the Mustard Plant

"What is the kingdom of God like? And to what should I compare it? It is like a mustard seed that someone took and sowed in the garden; it grew and became a tree, and the birds of the air made nests in its branches." (Luke 13:18-19, NRSV).

I gazed out my kitchen window at the expanse of lawn, evergreen trees, and shrubs—delightful greenery but no color. We had not set out any flowers, because they might wither while we were out of the city.

Then a new, sturdy plant began rising up rapidly beside the patio. Our neighbor said, "You are nurturing a wild weed. You might find mustard weeds springing up too freely." My husband asked, "Can't I pull out the weed for you?" "No, please, I want to see its flowers." In a few weeks the plant was four feet tall and sending out in all

95

directions thin stems holding erectly tiny yellow blossoms.

The total scene was an artist's delight—a huge bouquet swaying in the breeze. While working at my window, I admired the plant's tenacity. The flowers survived, fresh as ever, in excessive heat; they bowed submissively in heavy rain; they swayed flexibly when wind-blown.

I fantasized that the flowers were personalized posies. When I prayed for our nephew's pain after surgery, I liked to suppose the posies were bowing in sympathy. When our young neighbor left for missionary teaching in Mexico, I imagined the flowers were swaying cheerily in praise.

The spray of stems and flowers were functional as well as ornamental. Honey bees and white butterflies nibbled on their petals; the leaves can be cooked for food; its blossoms dry into seeds for the next generation of plants. The stems grew longer until the flowers were bending in their elderly stage. The bouquet became a tangled maze with the blossoms turning brown at the edges. Since I didn't want wild weeds to creep up on our neighbors' lawns, I asked my husband to chop down the thick stalk.

I drew a lesson for life from the mustard plant, a lesson about tenacity, flexibility, recovery, and usefulness. I am glad that God created color with which to teach us, and provides it abundantly in flowers and all of creation. God knew a black and white world would not be as cheerful, and so God created in us an aesthetic nature to enjoy the color of flowers, the background of green foliage, and the overhead canopy of blue sky.

Creator of all living things, your positioning the miracle plant exactly where I could view it while working shows your gracious response even to unvoiced desires. Thank you.

—⚬⚬⚬—

A Faithful Witness

"You will be my witnesses." (Acts 1:8, NRSV)

The setting was a converted Quonset hut that served as the officers' club at a remote United States Air Force base in northern Japan. The occasion was an officers' wives club Christmas tea to introduce American Christmas customs to a group of distinguished ladies from the neighboring Japanese city. Sapporo had a population of eighty thousand, with three Christian churches totaling fewer than three hundred members.

Upon arrival, I thought to myself that we were probably communicating that an American Christmas consisted of lavish decorations, more elegant baked goods than an army could eat, and some highly competitive drinking.

I had been asked to lead in the singing of some carols. We began with "Jingle Bells" and proceeded to "Winter

Wonderland." We dreamed of a "White Christmas" and celebrated Rudolph and Frosty. Then, recognizing the Japanese respect for history and speaking slowly through an interpreter, I made a transition. "Christmas," I explained, "is far more than a winter festival. It is the day when Christian people around the world celebrate the birth of Jesus Christ, whom they believe to be the Son of God and the Savior of all who believe. The most beautiful of the Christmas music is that which expresses their faith and worship." We then sang some of the real carols.

As I drew the program to a close, an elderly Japanese woman whom I knew to be a Christian walked toward me. "Buttry-San, may I sing a solo?" "Certainly, Mrs. Endo. What would you like to sing?" "Jesus Loves Me," she responded.

"Oh, Harriet, I can't play that!" came from the pianist. "Move over," I replied. "I can." So Mrs. Endo sang, first in Japanese and then in English, that wonderful song we learned as children. Her faithful witness said more about the meaning of Christmas than the planners of the tea had ever intended!

Lord, please help us to be faithful witnesses to the matchless love of Jesus. Amen.

JACQUIE CLINGAN

God's Handiwork

"So do not be afraid; you are of more value than many sparrows." (Matthew 10:31, NRSV)

A favorite spot in our home is a picture window that overlooks our back yard and a wooded area. Any time of day or any season gives a different picture. Autumn brings many colored leaves. Winter's tree branches become white with snow. Spring and summer bring new life, rich flowers aglow with color, and new dreams to explore.

How can anyone doubt the presence of God after seeing the beauty of creation, whether it is a plant, a flower, an animal, or a human being? David expressed it so beautifully in Psalm 19:1 (NRSV) with these words:

The heavens are telling the glory of God;
and the firmament proclaims his handiwork.

As I sit watching the birds I find myself singing, God's "eye is on the sparrow, and I know he watches me."

This morning there is a rose-breasted grosbeak in the tree. He hasn't come to the feeder but seems to be checking us out. A little wren is exploring the feeder. The cardinals and the blue jays go about their business as if to say, "Hey, this is our food—but you are welcome to share."

There are hyacinths that are almost covered by the bushes. They are in an area where we don't even see them unless we look for them. Yet, year after year, they continue to bloom in all their glory.

People are often like this. We miss their beauty because we don't take time to look. Do we stop to ask if they are frightened or full of stress? Do we offer a listening ear or a hand of friendship? How willing are we to reach out in compassion and say, "Hey, this is our food—but you are welcome to share"?

O God, help me to look beyond the beauty of your world to find both the needs and the beauty within those persons I encounter each day. Amen.

For the Record

> As Jesus was walking along, he saw a man called
> Matthew sitting at the tax booth; and he said to him,
> "Follow me." And he got up and followed him.
> (Matthew 9:9, NRSV)

My Scripture reading for the day was in Matthew's Gospel, the story of Jesus calling Matthew to be his disciple. "As Jesus was walking along, he saw a man called Matthew." I wonder how Matthew felt when he referred to himself by name as he made his calling a matter of historical record. I always feel strange referring to myself, either in a speech or in writing, by name or in the impersonal third person.

Someone may say that it just shows you that Matthew probably did not write the Gospel account that goes by his name. But let's assume that it was Matthew giving a personal account of his calling. Why would he use his name, rather than "I" or "me"? Considering what happened subsequently at his house—Jesus and his disciples having dinner with many tax collectors and other "sinners"—Matthew was saying, "Jesus came up to me; he found me and chose me to be his disciple; I, Matthew, a known social reject from my own people."

If something were written about me and made a public record—especially if I wrote it—I think that I would want it to be more flattering. But Matthew wasn't thinking of himself, but of Jesus and the message of God's love and acceptance. The story of Matthew teaches us that Jesus finds us, regardless of who we are—an outcast or a so-called good person. "Matthew got up and followed him." He relished Jesus' acceptance of him.

Jesus keeps finding me, wherever I may be. He showers me with his blessings of food and clothing and friends. Often when I am in my own world of thought or deed, he has a way of finding me and inviting me to follow him to his celebration of life. Like Matthew, it is because of Christ's grace that, whatever my story, I'll be happy to share it.

Loving God, thanks for finding me and calling me to belong to you. Amen.

JAN DeWITT

———⟨❀⟩———

Peter's Remedy for Stress

Cast all your anxiety on him, because he cares for
you. (1 Peter 5:7, NRSV)

Toward the end of his life Peter wrote these words to
Christians who were facing unbelievable persecution.
Peter was able to write these words because he had learned
that there is not a concern we have that we cannot give
over to the Lord. If I were to use two words to describe
Peter in his early years, they would be impulsive and pas-
sionate. But something happened that changed his character radically.

One Sunday our family camp learned, in a dramatic
way, what caused Peter to change. Our plan was to walk
along the shore as a group until we came upon a man
dressed as Jesus who was looking out at the lake. Peter was
to be brought to shore in a rowboat, and Jesus was to ask

him to join him. But God had other plans. Instead, the man who was playing the role of Peter impulsively jumped out of the boat and swam to shore. Everyone watched in amazement as he threw himself at the feet of the man called Jesus, saying, "Can you ever forgive me for denying you?" The man who was to be Jesus left his script and speaking from his heart said, "Of course I will; you're my friend." Then Peter said, "Can you really forgive me?" and Jesus said, "I not only forgive you but am giving you a mission—go feed my sheep."

From that moment on, the apostle Peter showed deliberate courage even when facing imprisonment. It was Peter who became the encourager of those facing Roman persecution and was able to write words he knew were true, "Cast all your cares on him, for he cares for you." Peter intentionally used two different words for "care" in this passage. The first meant "anxieties," and the second meant literally "our Lord will take charge of them"!

Lord, we thank you that we can give you all our cares and that you will take charge of them. No longer do we have to carry them alone. Amen.

Beatrice C. Fuller

—◦◦◦—

God Does Answer Prayer

"Whatever you ask for in prayer with faith, you will receive." (Matthew 21:22, NRSV)

My grandson, Jason, was knocked down by a sport-utility vehicle on Route 197 in Maryland. He was taken by helicopter to the Children's Medical Center, where he remained in surgery six hours for a broken femur, wrists, and pelvis.

I was almost en route to church when I received the news of the accident. My response: "Lord, help us!" I proceeded to church and asked for prayers for Jason's recovery. I prayed as I never have before. Jason's guardian angel must have been with him, because he could have been killed. God is good and does answer prayers, because in four months, Jason was walking again. I was brought up in a Christian home where I was taught to love God and Jesus early in life. Sunday school and church were ongoing things in our family. I naturally responded to what I had learned as a child. I was taught that God does answer prayer—just ask.

God does hear prayers. How God answers is another point. But I have faith that he will answer. Sometimes we wait, but patience is a discipline that brings us closer to the Master. He is the potter, and we are the clay. And prayer is such an elementary thing; it would behoove all of us to use it for the betterment of all.

Jason goes to church only when I take him, but we talk often by phone and I've tried to guide him in learning the Ten Commandments, which are God's rules for living, and the Beatitudes, which help persons go straight.

Thank you, God, for the many blessings you have bestowed upon us through our answered prayers. Amen.

VERNETTE F. FULOP, AS TOLD BY ROBERT E. FULOP

—◦◦◦◦—

I'm Hooked!

And he said to them, "Follow me, and I will make you
fish for people." (Matthew 4:19, NRSV)

"Why do you like fishing so much?" my wife asked one
night as I unloaded my fishing gear from the van. It was
dark, and she had been anxiously waiting for me, hoping I
hadn't fallen in the lake.

Why do I? I asked myself. I seldom bring home many
fish. When my dad died and left his tackle boxes and rods,
I set them on a basement shelf. I had no interest. When we
moved, I took them along since we had a lake nearby.

One day while cleaning the basement, I ran across the
stuff. Maybe I ought to try before I toss it away, I thought.

My teaching career was enjoyable but mind consum-
ing. After one busy day, I came home and thought I would
try fishing to relax. I went out to buy worms. I wasn't sure I

could work with the fancy flies or lures in the tackle boxes.

I got a few bites, but the fish slipped away. Yet it was fun. The routine was to throw in the line with a worm, let the fish nibble, and hope for a catch. Easy!

And so I became hooked. Even if I bring home an empty pail, it's always a pleasant experience. On good days, I filet the fish, and we enjoy a fresh fish dinner.

My wife considers herself a fish widow sometimes, so I have asked her to accompany me. Occasionally she does, and now she understands that out at the lake the sky is reflected in the water and it stays light much longer.

I find the best time to get a strike is at dusk, when the cool breezes come, the water is quiet, and the world takes on a hush. I enjoy the clouds, the moon rising over the trees, and the noisy crickets. Sometimes I see large fish jump out of the water, and it always tantalizes me.

I enjoy thinking and praying while I fish. I think of how Jesus called some of his disciples from along the shores of Galilee, of how he taught them to fish. Then he asked his followers to become fishers of people. My love of fishing connects me to his world and my calling as a minister to be a fisher of human beings. How wonderful to be a part of God's fishing expedition.

Lord Jesus, thank you for the reminder that, to be a fisher, one must be patient and creative. This also applies to being fishers of men and women. Patience in love and creative new approaches will ensure success in relating people to you, a loving and caring God. And there should be no empty pails. Amen.

LINN HORN

———⟡⟡⟡———

Surprise! God's Talking to You

> After the earthquake came a fire, but the Lord was not in the fire. And after the fire came a gentle whisper. When Elijah heard it, he pulled his cloak over his face and went out and stood at the mouth of the cave. (1 Kings 19:12-13, NIV)

When God speaks to people, it may not be like Candid Camera, but we may be surprised—by both how and what God has to say. If we hear him, it's a good idea to be like Elijah—and listen.

Late one night I was set for good intellectual exercise as I prepared to lead Bible study for my women's circle. I've forgotten the topic of the day, but an auxiliary Scripture transformed me and, ultimately, our family life.

At age thirty, armed with a sense of obligation, I kept a packed calendar with family tucked in around the edges.

The unexpected birth of a third baby sidelined me momentarily, but I returned to the habits that characterize the socially responsible. For my own well-being, my husband had asked me to slow down. However, because of my resolute personality, I ignored him and hurried on with life.

"Whoever knows what is right to do and fails to do it, for him it is sin" (James 4:17, RSV). The words were incidental to the study theme, yet they blindsided me and went to my core. God was talking to me—about listening to my husband! "But, Lord, what could he know? Jim's not spiritual!" These and more protestations raced through my head, but "knows ... right" ran faster and called more loudly.

Learning the lesson will take my lifetime. Listening to my husband isn't natural or easy. However, after God talked to me, I came home and learned to treasure the family he had entrusted to me, the family that often before had seemed to hinder important work. Both intellect and spirit were exercised through Bible study, and I learned to serve church and community with better judgment. Furthermore, I learned to relax occasionally. The last thirty years have been fun and satisfying beyond imagination. Our children are delightful, committed Christians. I'd like to think that they and the kingdom of God have profited from my decision to listen when the Lord (and Jim) talked.

Elijah had looked for the Lord in great and powerful events, but God's unexpected and gentle whisper caused him to listen. God's unexpected word caused me to listen and to accept counsel from a surprise source. Whenever advice conforms to and is confirmed by Holy Scripture, we can depend upon reward if we listen and accept that advice.

Lord, you've been talking to me again lately. The sources don't seem spiritual or powerful, but I know what is right. May I have the wisdom to do it. Thank you for talking to me. Amen.

W. KENNETH JACKSON

———✦✦✦———

Ride Tall in the Saddle

Keep alert, stand firm in your faith, be courageous, be strong. (1 Corinthians 16:13, NRSV)

I was born in 1917. As a young lad, I frequently heard it said about a person of good moral character, "He rides tall in the saddle." In those years horses were still used as a mode of transportation, and the adage harbored deep meaning.

We should live our lives in such a way that all people with whom we associate can look to us and know that we are Christians. Let Christ be in you to the extent that your faith shows in your face, your smile, your stance, your walk, and your talk.

In my working years I supervised up to 150 men at CF&K Steel Corporation in Pueblo, Colorado. When I retired, one person said to me, "I am a better man today because of having worked with you." What greater reward could we expect in life than to be told that we have lived our life in a way that inspired others to become better persons?

Ride tall in the saddle. Stand fast. Be strong, so that people may learn Christ through you.

Dear God of strength and honor, guide me that I may live my life in such a way as to be an example for others to follow. Amen.

NANCY KARO JOHNSON

—◦◦◦—

"She Has Done What She Could"

"She has done what she could; she has anointed my body beforehand for its burial." (Mark 14:8, NRSV)

She walked in, and the men glared. How dare she! She wasn't invited, and she surely wasn't welcome. Actually, she was forbidden to enter. "Despised" would describe our reaction to her. This was for men only! She knew that.

Our leader will put her in her place. Just watch.

Slowly, deliberately, almost reverently, she came in, walking directly toward our leader. She didn't look to her left or to her right. It was as though we were invisible, as if no one else was in the room. She wasn't curious about her surroundings and didn't seem to care what we might do to her. She wasn't anxious, only determined.

116

Much to our consternation, our leader didn't get angry. He didn't tell her she was intruding and not welcome. He didn't tell her to leave.

He only returned her gaze—with respect.

That woman, that uninvited, unwelcome, law-shirking woman, then had the gall to take expensive perfume (we could tell by the rich aroma that it was costly) and pour it over him.

What a waste! What a shame. Unconscionable. She could have sold it and given the money to the poor.

"Woman! You fool! Look at what you have done. Why are you wasting this expensive perfume? Don't you know we could have sold it and helped the poor? Get out of here, or we'll throw you out!"

But our leader stood up and looked at us with a mixture of pity and sadness. "Why must you make trouble for her? It is a fine thing she has done for me. You have the poor among you always, and you can help them whenever you like; but you will not always have me" (Mark 14:6-7, NEB).

He turned and put his hand on her. Looking back at us, Jesus said, "She has done what she could." His look said, "What have you done for me?"

God, thank you for your respect for us—for loving us when others do not care and do not respect or honor us. Sometimes we need to "waste" ourselves on you, even though others will criticize. Help us not to fall into the traps of disrespect, criticism, and condemnation. It is so easy to be caught up in being the best or doing more than anyone else and even being more spiritual than others instead of giving what we have to you. Help us to do what we can with what you have given us so we can hear you say, "She has done what she could." Amen.

Patricia A. Kohls

———✺———

Patience of Faith in Retirement

Be still before the Lord and wait patiently for him.
(Psalm 37:7, NIV)

On summer weekends my husband and I attend outdoor archery shoots at various cities. Each forest presents a new venture with a different terrain and vegetation. Every course challenges our talents in many ways. We quietly approach the station from where we will shoot. We focus on the target ahead gently holding the bow with an arrow in place. When releasing the arrow we trust it to speed straight to the target. If the arrow has a distance to go and a target is downhill, it might go above or below the target.

Like the bow and arrow is in the hands of an archer our retirement life is in the hands of God. This future target lies ahead of us, and God has pointed us to it. We wait patiently in God's presence knowing he has a purpose in his sight for us. Quietly God leads us toward it. We know the Lord will not forsake or leave us no matter what happens in our future.

We might be moving to another city, taking on a part-time job, starting a home improvement project, beginning a new hobby or recreational activity. During our retirement we may have many new experiences to adapt to. The course we are on could hold some distractions or physical setback that we might not predict or anticipate.

Some of our unfolding experiences are joy-filled with births or marriages within our families. We have been blessed with new friends and renewed friendships with faithful acquaintances in our encounters on life's paths.

Patience is a fruit of the Holy Spirit, which strengthens our soul during retirement, giving a quiet hope deep within our hearts. We wait in stillness of trusting faith and understanding patience, for our Lord to work, move, and act through us one day at a time.

Loving Lord, humbly we put our frail lives into your divine hands. Thank you for the gift of faith-filled patience to face all the challenges life has to offer in our retirement. Amen.

WILDA K. W. (WENDY) MORRIS

—◦◦◦—

Advent Wings

But the angel said to them, "Do not be afraid; for
see—I am bringing you good news of great joy for all
the people." (Luke 2:10, NRSV)

According to an ancient legend, birds originally didn't
have wings. The birds began to complain to one another
that they were small and weak compared with most of the
animals. The more they talked about it the more fearful
they became. So they went to God to discuss their fate.

"We are so vulnerable," the birds told God. "We don't
feel safe." God took their concerns seriously and gave them
wings. They thanked God and walked away.

But life didn't improve. Indeed, it seemed that God had
made matters worse by laying a burden of bone and feath-
ers on their backs. In a day or two, the birds returned to
God. "We told you we didn't feel safe," they said. "And you

made us more awkward and vulnerable, with these heavy things to carry."

"Oh," said God, "your wings are not intended to be burdens! If you learn to use them, they will help you fly."

Sometimes Advent is a burden of bone and feather. I find myself rushing and frazzled. It is easy to be cross with my children and grandchildren, my husband, coworkers, or friends—whoever crosses my path. I begin to wonder if decking the halls is worth the bother. The silver bells I hear along the street add to the cacophony of noise and make it hard to concentrate enough to remember everything I set out to do.

As cookies are baked, dirty dishes pile up. I drop a raw egg on the kitchen floor. There are cards to address, letters to answer, gifts to wrap. A scarf or a glove is missing. The driveway needs to be shoveled. I need to practice my part in the Christmas program. The phone rings, and someone asks me to add something else to an already overcrowded schedule.

Instead of singing carols, I want to cry.

When I calm down, I remind myself that Advent is not intended to be a burden. I ask God to teach me to use Advent as it was intended. Which things on my to-do list can be dropped or postponed—and which ones are really important? Which help me remember the good news of great joy proclaimed by the angels that first Christmas? Which are done from a sense of obligation and which take wing as acts of love?

Dearest Jesus, help me to fly this season of Advent. Let me be loving and joyful. Help me to concentrate on those things that honor you and express your compassion to others. Amen.

—◦◦◦—

A Lifetime of Sowing

"Still other seed fell on good soil, where it produced a crop—a hundred, sixty or thirty times what was sown." (Matthew 13:8, NIV)

From childhood through the retirement years of life, I have cultivated the soil, planted the seed, cared for the growing plants, and enjoyed the fresh produce grown in backyard gardens from Maine to Indiana. From God's call to ministry, through educational preparation, and out into the garden of life, I have planted the Word. I have rejoiced when the seed that is the Word found its way into the life of an individual and sprouted, began to grow, and brought forth a lovely Christian life.

The parable of the sower clearly indicates that as many as three out of four seeds fail to produce a crop, fail to meet the potential within the seed. Birds eat some of the seed, rocky soil prevents growth of other seed, and fast-growing weeds choke plants that managed to sprout. Jesus lets us know that it is this way with the Word that is sown.

I've sometimes found it easy to forget the arithmetic of this parable and to become discouraged when the Word I've sown seems to have failed to produce a crop. Some of those in whom the Word was sown ignored it, but this could be understood and accepted fairly easily. More discouraging were the times when some received the Word with enthusiasm and seemed to flourish but quickly wilted and left the fellowship. Others accepted the Word and started to grow, but gradually the busyness of their lives crowded it out, and they were lost to the cause of Christ. In all of this, it was easy to overlook those who received the Word and became strong, flourishing Christians.

During my first pastorate, we celebrated the fiftieth anniversary of the founding of the church. Fifty years later I was invited back to preach the one-hundredth-anniversary sermon. As the pastor brought the service to a close, he asked all who had been a part of the fiftieth anniversary to come to the front of the church. It was through tears of joy and thankfulness that I saw coming forward two sisters, the first persons I had baptized as a young pastor, plus many others who had confessed their faith in Christ, been baptized, and become members of the church. These were now parents and grandparents whose families are today a vital part of the fellowship of the church. The seed planted fifty years ago was still producing a bountiful crop.

This was a clear testimony to me: Our task is to plant the Word, and God provides the growth.

Continue to use me, Lord, in the wonderful task of sowing the Word and trusting you for growth. Amen.

Ministry in a Graveyard

And I heard a voice from heaven, saying, "Write this:
Blessed are the dead who from now on die in the
Lord." "Yes," says the Spirit, "they will rest from their
labors, for their deeds follow them." (Revelation
14:13, NRSV)

I had just arrived from New Jersey for my summer visit.
My ninety-three-year-old dad had been living with my
brother and his wife ever since Mom passed away in 1977.
Although I came to see Dad each year, I was worried about
this visit because, for in the last year or so, my father was
becoming increasingly fearful and depressed. He told me
he was thinking too much about dying. In his own words,
"I've been wonderin' about how much longer I'll be here.
And what passin' on would be like." Those can be depress-
ing thoughts for anyone.

127

Dad's depression was a complex issue for me, for Dad and I rarely talked much about spiritual things. As an experienced pastor, teacher, writer, and communicator, I was at ease sharing the gospel with almost everyone. But I was not very comfortable talking about Jesus with my own dad.

And here he was worried about dying, and I seemed to be unable to deal with it.

I prayed that God would give me an opportunity that summer to talk to my dad about death and the hope that Jesus holds out to all who believe. I wanted him to taste God's wonderful shalom peace in his final years, so that he could prepare himself to pass on with calm certainty and assurance. I was still praying that day as Dad and I talked while weeding around Mom's gravestone.

Then it happened—the opportunity.

The reference to Revelation 14:13 had been inscribed on Mom's headstone. And there it was so clear, for both of us to see. I pointed Dad to the text and asked him if he knew what the text meant: "Blessed are the dead who die in the Lord." He said he wasn't sure, so I swallowed hard and began to offer a short homily on the blessings and promise of God for all of us who believe and trust in him as we move toward our own time of passing.

Dad seemed to be more at peace as we drove back from the cemetery that summer day. He needed a word of peace and hope, and he got it from God's Word through me. The graveyard visit also helped me in several ways. First, it reminded me (again) of how God answers prayer, often in strange, wonder-filled ways. Second, it reminded me of the power of God's written Word and of its eternal relevance for all occasions. Last, it brought back to memory my own need for empowerment by the Spirit in order to offer effective love, care, and hope to those who are closest to me, even family and friends.

O living Lord, please teach us to remember the awesome power and to recognize your ever-creative and fresh ways of dealing with our deepest needs and the needs of those around us. Amen.

BARBARA SMITH

Epiphanies

> With all wisdom and insight he has made known to us the mystery of his will, according to his good pleasure that he set forth in Christ. (Ephesians 1:8-9, NRSV)

The letter read, "We would like you to write a twenty-page essay on epiphany in the writing of poetry." Writing is indeed a religious experience for me. It is the use of a God-given gift to share my experiences and those of others.

The epiphanies that occur in the act of writing are mysterious and wonderful. Their occasional appearance is what compels me as a writer to write.

But even as I have worked on the assigned essay, I have been newly aware of just how mysterious and wonderful are the ways of God. He works through me and through an unknown third-grader who sent me a sky poem that I will treasure forever. God works through sculptors and through the parent or teacher who encouraged that boy to write that poem and send it to me.

God works through grocery store clerks and the local school custodian. He works through the Bible lying close on this desk and through the thunderstorm crashing outside my window. And the wonder is that his works will never, ever end.

In addition to the Psalms, the poetry of Gerard Manley Hopkins is one of the best examples in all literature of epiphany in poetry. Surely such masterpieces as "God's Grandeur" and "Pied Beauty" are clear evidence. Or how about Emily Dickinson's work? Or William Blake's? Or John Donne's? The list is almost endless, going far back beyond the printed word and far forward to the end of history. And the miracle is that the epiphany can and does occur not just for the writer but for the reader as well. God does indeed work in mysterious ways. What a blessing!

Glory be to you, O God, for the wonder of our world, the beauty of each day, the mystery of your love as revealed to us in the words that we write and read, and most especially in our Lord Jesus Christ. Amen.

—◦◦◦—

As a Child

"Let the little children come to me, and do not stop
them; for it is to such as these that the kingdom of
heaven belongs." (Matthew 19:14, NRSV)

My husband, Jim, died in the month of October. The pre-
vious summer, our three-year-old granddaughter, Wendy,
spent hours playing near him as he sat in his recliner in the
living room. She poured him imaginary tea and gave him
imaginary pills. If he mistakenly drank the pill she scolded
him: "Grampa, that's a pill, that's not tea!" Wendy was having a bad time herself due to a long-term infection that
was as yet undiagnosed. Her energy level was low, and the
only time she seemed to feel comfortable was when she
was taking care of Grampa.

Wendy and her family returned to their own home at
the end of the summer, and the next time she came to our

house was at the time of Jim's funeral. We tried to explain to her that Grampa was in heaven, but of course that had little meaning or comfort for a three-year-old. She cried if anyone else sat in Grampa's chair. She was a mirror for all our suffering. My husband was a much-loved man.

The following winter was terrible for all of us. Our grief took various forms, but mostly we felt lost and joyless. My daughter, Wendy's mother, reported that Wendy barely dragged herself around. She came slowly downstairs each morning and couldn't eat her breakfast. Her infection had finally been diagnosed, but treatment didn't seem to be helping her lethargy much. She seldom smiled.

Then one morning about two months after Jim's death, Wendy came bounding down the stairs, her eyes shining and her face lit up like a Christmas tree.

"Momma, Momma," she said. She was so excited, she practically danced. "I saw Grampa last night."

"You did?" her mother said. "Where was that, Wendy?"

"He was at Jesus' house. And he was so happy."

We had never used the term "Jesus' house." We knew that Wendy really had seen something that night that comforted her—whether in a dream or a vision we don't know. But we too were comforted by it. The reassurance that

Wendy received helped the whole family. And it reminded us that unless we change and become as little children, we won't be able to receive the promises of the kingdom.

Good Shepherd, keep reminding us that we need to keep a childlike trust and faith in you. Amen.

Joy versus Happiness

"If you keep my commandments, you will abide in my love, just as I have kept my father's commandments and abide in his love. I have said these things to you so that my joy may be in you, and that your joy may be complete." (John 15:10-11, NRSV)

Someone gave me a plaque with a picture of a little girl holding a sheet of music and singing, "Now is the time to be happy." At another time in my life I would have welcomed this gift and not given the verse another thought. But I had been going through a sad experience, and the plaque only intensified my feelings of sadness.

I wondered what kind of response I would receive if I were to give my plaque to someone who had just lost a loved one, or to an elderly person whose circumstances required moving into a nursing home. The scenarios were endless, but one thing was certain. I had to find answers to my questions before I would have any peace.

I began by looking up the word *happy* in the dictionary. I found that "happy" comes from the root word *hap*, meaning "chance or luck, favored by circumstances." As a Christian I believe that there is no such thing as luck, that God has a plan for our lives, and when we trust in him, nothing is left to chance.

When I looked up the word *happy* in the Bible concordance, I found only six references in the New Testament. But when I looked up the word *joy,* I found sixty-three references.

The Scripture that interested me most was Matthew 28:8 (NIV), "So the women hurried away from the tomb, afraid yet filled with joy." I came to the conclusion that even when we are sad or fearful, we can still have joy in our hearts. Unlike happiness, which depends on outward circumstances such as good health and pleasant surroundings, joy comes from the inside.

Thank you, Jesus, for the gift of joy. Thank you for opening my eyes to the truth that even when we suffer trials and heartaches in this life you will fill us with a joy that only you can give. Amen.

136

—◦◦◦—

The Need of a Mediator

Jesus said to him, "I am the way, the truth, and the life. No man comes to the Father except through Me." (John 14:6, NKJV)

Our group of eleven was touring the sunny isle of Cyprus in June before the wedding of our Cypriot protégé and her American fiancé. They were our tour guides along the blue Mediterranean Sea.

After seeing the picturesque harbor and famous mosaics of Paphos and the St. Neophytos Monastery, we started back with our car of five following the other car of six, carrying the bride and groom, the only ones who knew the tour route.

After twenty minutes of driving, the groom's father said, "I have not seen the other car for awhile." On we went to Paphos, then up and down and around, still searching.

137

Nighttime brought a drizzling rain, and the groom's parents suggested we register at the nearest hotel.

During all the searching, I was analyzing how the separation problem could be solved in future trips. One method would require the two drivers to secure a mediator before leaving home base. The first driver would phone the mediator or link person, who would name the place to meet. When the other driver called, he would be given that message.

We five were getting settled in our hotel rooms when the groom telephoned, "Finally, I've found you after calling several hotels! Evidently you lost sight of us when we angled off the road to take a photo."

I saw a spiritual parallel to this experience. We have a Mediator if we should become alienated from God. We can lose sight of him due to extreme busyness, worldly distractions, or postponement of communication. Jesus said that no one comes to the Father except through him, but the wonder of that statement is that Jesus does make a way to the Father.

Father God, we thank you for our Mediator, Jesus, who redeemed us by his supreme sacrifice and guides us on the highway to eternity. Amen.

Linn Horn

———⟨ဏ⟩———

Garden in the Woods

And let us not grow weary while doing good, for in due season we shall reap if we do not lose heart. (Galatians 6:9, NKJV)

"I'll bet you spend a lot of time meditating out here in all this beauty." Mary Ann's warm smile conveyed her appreciation for our place in the woods, but her comment revealed how busy she'd been as a single mother of six. She had never gardened in the woods.

Writing at the picnic table the other day, I recounted the effort it took to snatch rest from Ohio's encircling green. There were days of weeding, seeding, potting and repotting, hose hauling, brick cleaning, hole digging, planting and replanting and—pain-pill popping. My picnic-table vision of heaven in May allows only brief respite from the woodland wars. Every day offers new battlegrounds with encroaching plants or animals, all doing what is only natural to them and anathema to the gardener—me! Coarse, innumerable plants with microscopic blooms, irritating leaves, deep roots, and too many seeds prosper where I want the grace and beauty of lilies and daisies. The raccoons and chipmunks rip out whatever grows in improved soil. It seems they think the good stuff is for them only.

The next day my time of outdoor writing was delayed while I tenderly repotted baby annuals. They had been ripped from soil where they could thrive and were wantonly scattered over the patio floor. Some had been mortally wounded; others might recover.

Today I am delighted by a soft breeze, iris, columbines, hostas, daylilies, roses, and hummingbirds at the feeder. Today I am reminded that the moment is fleeting. For if leisure is long, the bed straws, poison ivy, crabgrass, thistles, deer, raccoons, squirrels, chipmunks, and ground hogs—all natural to our back yard—will have their way with my source of inspiration.

And so it is for Christians, being the church on earth. We can exult in worship and powerful preaching. We can luxuriate in each other's company. By nature those moments are fleeting. Just as woodland gardeners must be persevering, so we the church must be diligent. We must guard the vision of the church, support and uphold our pastors and leaders in prayer, and care for new and tender family members. If we allow ourselves to grow weary, the strength of secular society—the coarse, common, rank, and hardy elements of all that is only natural to humanity—will surely overgrow God's garden in the woods, the church on earth.

O Lord, our Lord, let us not lose heart. Encourage us in the midst of battle. Amen.

WILDA K. W. (WENDY) MORRIS

———✿✿✿———

Behind the Annoyances— Blessings

Give thanks in all circumstances; for this is the will of God in Christ Jesus for you. (1 Thessalonians 5:18, NRSV)

Thanksgiving dinner was over. I washed dishes. My oldest granddaughter, Barb, dried them. My daughter Sherri supervised three other grandchildren as they put pickles and olives back in the jars and brought dishes from the dining room to the kitchen. As we worked, I began to notice an unpleasant smell. I realized there was water in the sink under the dish rack and assumed the plug was blocking the rinse water from running out. I decided it was time for clean dishwater, so I pulled the plug. It didn't drain quickly, so I started the disposal. Suddenly there was more water in the other side of the sink. I realized that it was the source of the odor. There was a blockage in the sewer line.

The next time someone needed a toilet, they went to the main-floor bathroom, because my husband was sure the blockage had not affected it. Wrong! The toilet ran over. There I was on Thanksgiving, mopping up the over-flow. Fortunately, as soon as the toilet had flooded the floor, the blockage was released, and the toilet flushed properly. The malodorous water drained from the kitchen sink, and the plumbing was back to normal. My children and grandchildren left because they had other plans for the evening. There I was—much later—cleaning the bathroom and kitchen and rewashing and sterilizing the dishes and silverware.

In the evening someone called and asked if we had a nice Thanksgiving. I sighed but then realized how much we had to be thankful for that day! We had two of our five children and four of our grandchildren with us. We had enjoyed Thanksgiving dinner before the plumbing malfunctioned. We have indoor plumbing—even if it gives us problems occasionally. The problem righted itself, so we did not have the expense of calling a plumber on a holiday. We have floors to mop, not just dirt floors. We have pots and pans, dishes and silverware that were worth washing a second time and sterilizing.

It is easy to focus on the things that go wrong from day to day. But if we realize how blessed we are, we live with more joy!

Make a list of little annoyances you have experienced recently. After each one, list the blessings without which you would not have had the annoyance. Then thank God for each of those blessings.

Our Clay Vessels

The Perfect Pot

A PARABLE

The letter said, "We want you to come to our seniors' night and talk to us about aging, especially about being productive in retirement."

That didn't sound too difficult. After all, I had written my doctoral dissertation on the subject of retirement adjustment. Naturally, I had quite a bit to say on the subject! But when I sat down to write those things, the speech wouldn't come out right. And then this old potter entered my heart, and I knew I had to tell his story—because it was really **our** story.

Once upon a time in a far off country that you've never heard of before, there lived a very old potter. In his youth he heard a legend from a passing peddler: If anyone shapes

146

and molds something perfect with his or her own efforts, and then gives it as an offering on God's altar, that person will please God and have eternal life.

"But how will anyone know if it's perfect or not?" asked the potter.

"If it isn't perfect, then the moment it touches the altar, it will be destroyed. Nothing that isn't just the way God wants it may touch the altar of God."

Believing what he was told, the goal of the potter's life from that day onward was to please God and therefore have eternal life. Each year he selected the most beautiful pot that he could find among his creations. He wound his way up the long hill to the temple and there offered his pot upon the altar. And each year the beautiful creation slowly developed cracks and fell to pieces on the altar.

Undaunted by this failure, the potter went back to his wheel and began again, praying with each turn of the wheel and each firing of the kiln that this would indeed be the creation that would please God and bring him eternal life.

The villagers all knew of his efforts. And they profited greatly from it. His pots were known far and wide for their beauty and utility. No pot of his ever cracked when filled with boiling soup—nor did it look ugly sitting out all day.

His creations were prized family treasures, passed on as heirlooms in families and even quarreled over by jealous siblings after a parent's death.

And every year with the regularity of the seasons, the potter toiled yet once more up the long hill to the temple, laying yet another beautiful creation on the altar. And each year he came down a little older, a little more stooped, yet still determined that one day his offering would be pleasing to God.

On the day of offering, the villagers were particularly kind to the potter. He was so patient and good-natured about his annual failures. They loved him for his efforts to please God, and all prayed that he would one day attain his goal. He inspired many of the younger workers to begin making trips to the altar with their creations, and soon the temple was visited many times during the year. Children loved him for his kind smile and willingness to help them make beautiful new creations.

The years moved on. The potter's struggle up the hill took longer and longer each year. His hands, once so agile and strong, could no longer knead the clay and pull it off center to make a pot. He no longer had beautiful pots to take with him to the temple.

So on this morning, the potter struggled up the hill for the last time. He had no pot to offer. This time he was going to ask God why no pot of his had ever pleased God, so that now, in his old age, he was denied eternal life.

The potter sensed a difference as he approached the altar. He had never touched the altar itself before, but this time he extended both his hands out on the altar hoping to get God's attention. As his hands rested on the altar, he thought he could feel a hand on his head and a soft voice sighing, "I am well pleased!"

Those who saw the old potter come down from the temple knew something had happened. His face shone with happiness and joy. He tried to tell people about touching the altar, about the sound of singing, about the voice, but they thought it just the wandering of an old mind.

The old potter is long gone now, but if you visit that village today, you will see people struggling up the hill to lay their creations on the altar. All the work done in that village is of the highest quality. No one has yet reported that God accepted a single crafted item as pleasing and perfect. Yet all who struggle up the hill, having nothing but *themselves* to offer come down the hill with shining faces and never feel the need to make the trip again.

—∞∞∞—

Decisions

"I call heaven and earth today to witness against you:
I have set before you life and death, the blessing and
the curse. Choose life, then, that you and your
descendants may live, by loving the Lord, your God."
(Deuteronomy 30:19-20, NAB)

A nasty little bug moved slowly across my writing pad.
What a distraction, I thought as I got up to grab a paper
towel off the rack next to the table. I was determined to rid
myself of the pesky intruder. As I hovered over it, my hand
cast a shadow. Immediately the small bug must have
detected the impending danger, because it quickly flipped
on its back and played dead. I stood still; the little rascal by
its actions showed me it wanted to live. Gently I picked up
the bug and placed it outside.

So many times when a dark shadow falls across my

path, I too want to curl up and play dead. But God in his infinite mercy sends someone or something into my life to rescue me.

As the youngest child in my family I've dealt with the deaths of my parents and four of my siblings. During the latest losses (two were just months apart) I became grief-stricken, and the davenport became my haven from the storm. I feared I'd never get over the pain. The intense sorrow stole my zeal for life. Early one morning, my long-time friend Claudia called and detected in my voice a sadness I was unable to hide. She asked if she could come over and sit with me. Not wanting to be alone, I said yes. Claudia stayed all day, listening to me talk about my fears of never feeling normal again. Occasionally she interjected a word of comfort, but mostly she listened. Finally she said, "Caye, I believe you have a broken heart." Those words made me aware of what I was dealing with. I realized I needed healing, and in the grieving process, healing takes time. I was not allowing myself that time. In saying yes to my friend's concern for me that day, I chose life.

God's love is constantly present. It may be in a conversation with one of my friends or in a Scripture reading for the day that will have the exact words I need to hear.

Sometimes just sitting in silence with the Lord frees me to see my situation in a new perspective. Life or death is always my choice.

My Lord, Creator of all life, each day I am faced with decisions of life or death, blessings or curses. So, I surrender myself into your loving care, and by doing this, I choose life and blessings. Amen.

—◦◦◦—

Isolation and Grace

Like good stewards of the manifold grace of God,
serve one another with whatever gift each of you has
received. (1 Peter 4:10, NRSV)

Lois and I returned from working out at the club to find
the message light blinking on our answering machine.
While she fixed lunch, I listened to a young woman rat-
tling off something or other in a lilting soprano voice. It's
not uncommon for me to miss a few words of such
recordings, but this lady was unintelligible. I touched the
replay button but still couldn't make any sense out of her
rapid-fire happy talk.

Unwilling to yield to an idiot recording machine, I
turned up both hearing aids and again hit replay. The voice
was certainly louder, but alas, still no comprehension. As a
last resort, I asked Lois to see if she could understand the

message. For her, just one time through was sufficient—I was one of the few, select individuals eligible for yet another pre-approved credit card.

Accepting deterioration of good hearing has been hard for me. I feel a growing sense of isolation, even rejection, when those around me laugh at a joke but I didn't catch the punch line. Pride causes me to laugh anyway, just to camouflage my embarrassment.

It's hard to accept increasing dependency on someone's help for the little, everyday things that make life interesting and fun. But I've come to believe that such freely given help is a gift from God.

And every gift needs a receiver; that's the moment when grace occurs.

I'll try to remember that with the next unintelligible voice message.

Dear Lord, help me joyfully accept the gift of assistance as my five senses diminish with age. I want to share your grace with folks blessed with the gift of knowing how to help others. Amen.

Harriet Arnold Buttry

—◦◦◦—

It's Always Too Soon to Quit

Those who wait for the Lord shall renew their strength,
    they shall mount up with wings like eagles,
they shall run and not be weary,
    they shall walk and not faint.
(Isaiah 40:31, NRSV)

It was the day after my mother's funeral when we found her note on a slip of paper marking the last book she had been reading. A list headed "Look up these words" was barely legible because of the arthritis that had grotesquely deformed her hands. Her last days had been spent almost entirely in her bedroom and sitting room at my sister's home. An avid reader, my mother was mentally alert and curious to the end. The dictionary was at the other end of

155

the house, where she only got occasionally. We looked at the book, saw how deeply thoughtful and challenging it was, and realized that this wonderful woman was still learning and growing at the age of eighty-four.

As I thought about that, a memory from college surfaced. Our basketball team was playing a top team from a larger school. By halftime it looked like we were going to be clobbered. In the second half, however, our players started nibbling away at that big lead. The tension and enthusiasm built as the clock wound down and our team tied the score at the buzzer. It took two overtimes, but we won! At chapel the next day, our college president drew some lasting spiritual lessons on the topic. It's always too soon to quit.

Those memories faded as the years rushed by until I was left a widow at age fifty-one. About nine months after my husband's death, I felt an unmistakable leading from God to return to school—seminary, to be more specific. After some struggle, I gave in and claimed the verse from Isaiah as my own. So I began theological studies as a middle-aged, widowed grandmother, attending classes with people about the ages of my sons. I wasn't sure I had the physical or mental energy to continue. Then the pictures would come back—

of a basketball team that demonstrated that it's always too soon to quit, and especially of my crippled, eighty-four-year-old mother still learning and growing. I learned from her the truth especially of walking and not fainting—just keeping going in the strength God supplies.

Lord, help us to keep on growing as we draw on your strength one day at a time. Amen.

M. Dosia Carlson

———◦◦◦———

All of Me

Or do you not know that your body is a temple of the
Holy Spirit? (1 Corinthians 6:19, NKJV)

When I was a child, my parents helped me remain healthy.
They took me to Dr. Nagle for annual physical checkups.
He was a congenial family doctor who smelled like bleach.

Whenever I visited his office, I knew I would be
rewarded by choosing my favorite flavor of sucker. Even
though at times he hurt me, such as by giving me typhoid
shots before I went to Girl Scout camp, I didn't mind going
to see him. Dr. Nagle made my earache go away, and he
was sorry when my kitten died.

As I have grown older, my experience with physicians
has changed. So has the industry of health care. Our society bombards us with all kinds of information about how
to care for our bodies. No longer can we assume that there

is a family doctor waiting to treat any ailment we may have. Although there are many dedicated doctors, our system too often limits time for in- depth patient contact. And the marvel of modern technology means that in seeking wellness, our bodies may be seeing machines more than health care providers.

Moreover, the medical profession is chopping up our bodies into smaller and smaller subspecialties. When consulting one orthopedic specialist about knee pain, I ventured a question about discomfort in my shoulder. He informed me, "I don't do upper extremities."

So who is helping us understand the importance of integrating body, mind, and spirit? Fortunately, the parish nurse movement is fostering a holistic approach to caring for the temple of the Holy Spirit. In our congregation Linda Carlson Shaw, R.N., provides such basic services as semi-monthly blood pressure checks.

Predominantly older people, but members of all ages, flock to the health ministry office for these checkups.

Linda also visits men and women in their homes to discuss such concerns as depression, community resources, and family problems. Through exercise classes and other approaches she offers ways for people to remain healthy. Instead of ending a visit with a lollipop, she shares God's strength through prayer. What a blessing to know that our faith can make us whole.

Source of life and love, we thank you for the miracle of our bodies. Help us to discover and use ways of being in partnership with you for wholeness of our physical, emotional, and spiritual selves. Amen.

———⟨ονν⟩———

Affirming the Move

Give instruction to the wise,
    and they will become wiser still.
(Proverbs 9:9, NRSV)

"I don't want to move," my friend confessed to me. She was in her late eighties. "My children think I need to enter a senior residence. I want to stay here, where my husband and I enjoyed our retirement years together. I love all the flowers we planted. They make summer such a joy. I have so many wonderful memories. I'm getting along okay. My neighbors look in on me. The grandchildren stop by several times a week. My daughter checks in. I don't think I need to move yet. Maybe someday."

I listened to my friend. She continued to give reason after reason why she should stay in her home. Never once did she refer to the fact that living by herself was becoming more of a challenge to her and more of a burden to others. She had fallen more than once. She seemed determined to stay.

Over the next few months I watched and listened as my friend continued to resist the pressure of her adult children. Their negotiations reached a new level when an apartment became available in the senior residence. The children insisted that their mother cooperate with their plan and prepare for the move. Reluctantly my friend put her beloved house on the market. She selected the belongings she would take with her. She gave other things away. Finally the day came when she made the move. I could tell it was very hard for her. The first few weeks in her new setting were a challenge. She struggled to be positive and optimistic.

About six months later I went to visit my friend. She greeted me radiantly. "God has been so good to bring me here," she declared. She went on to talk about the friends she joined regularly for her main meal. She spoke about the security she experienced in knowing people checked on her daily. "When the time comes, I can move to assisted living and even to the nursing home, if I need it. I'm so blessed to be here."

I reminded her of her earlier resistance. She grinned, "They were wiser than I. I think deep inside I knew they were right. It was just so hard to move out of my home. Now I'm so glad I did it." She laughed. "Maybe I should have done it earlier." We chuckled together.

Today my friend, now in her nineties, is a volunteer visitor in the residence nursing home. She assists newcomers in meeting the other residents. She leads a weekly Bible study in her small apartment.

O God, help us to listen to the wisdom of those close to us—especially when they see more clearly than we do the decisions we need to make. Amen.

———∞∞∞———

Let Them Go

"Unbind him, and let him go." (John 11:44, RSV)

The Pennsylvania Dutch have a saying: "Too soon old, too late smart." I find it coming to mind more often as I approach retirement age.

During the years before my mother died, I took time to collect oral history about our family. I had heard bits and pieces as I grew up, but I found the details set in a larger context fascinating. However, Mom often turned the conversation to more personal issues. She was struggling with junk that seemed to be crowding out good memories. An old struggle with her sister for her mother's attention kept coming up in our conversations. She never felt good enough in her mother's eyes when compared with her sister.

After getting over my surprise that my self-confident mother was really troubled inside, I began to listen more carefully and help her talk out the issues. It was not too late to deal with them and find release.

I have become aware that there is old junk in my life that troubles me from time to time. I realize that just because I'm older doesn't mean it's too late to look for help in working out old issues.

Lazarus had been in the grave for four days when Jesus called him to new life. Take note! Jesus chose not to do all the work to bring new life to Lazarus. He invited, no, directed the people present to loose Lazarus from the grave clothes that bound him. Jesus trusts ministry to people such as pastors, counselors, friends, and family. It is not too late to ask for help.

Nor is it too late for us to be present for other persons who are looking for new life. Jesus reported that God's intent is that we experience life abundant, which is not restricted to any age.

God, may we have the courage to ask for help and the grace to offer it to others for Jesus' sake. Amen.

Faith: Victory Over Crisis

Let us run with perseverance the race that is set
before us, looking to Jesus the pioneer and perfecter
of our faith. (Hebrews 12:1-2, NRSV)

I was finishing a strenuous but fruitful interim ministry
when I became troubled with physical problems—lack of
balance, dizziness, and abnormal fatigue.

Was it my age? After all, I was seventy-two and not
fifty-two. Did I have a fatal disease? My wife said, "See
your doctor!"

My doctor ordered an MRI. I received the report within a week and was shocked to learn that it showed a tumor
wrapped around my pituitary gland. My neurosurgeon
explained that the pituitary gland does much more than
affect one's growth. It controls the whole hormone system
of the body. Even after surgery, I would need to be under

the care of an endocrinologist for the rest of my life.

Immediately I realized that I needed to ask myself, "How strong is my faith? Am I willing to turn all things over to my God and my Lord Jesus Christ? Or will I in fear try to fight the battle by myself?" After a struggle, I admit, I determined to place my faith in God. I had to trust that when I did, no matter what I faced, all would be well.

What a comfort and peace I felt! I received word that along with the prayers of my family, prayers were being lifted up for me through the congregations for which I had pastored over the fifty years of my ministry. Prayers were being lifted up for me in other congregations, even of other faiths, through the National Interfaith Coalition on Aging and through many friends who wanted to undergird me and express their love.

And I felt those prayers! At the time of my surgery, I was at peace and felt the closeness of my God and my Lord. I knew that the hands of the surgeons and the nurses were being guided by the God of love and healing. The result was in many ways miraculous. All of the negatives that the surgeons said could happen as a result of the surgery never happened. And the tumor was benign.

I was truly in God's hands.

So, when you face a crisis, depend upon your Christian faith. Trust in the God who loves you. No matter what you face, even defeat, perhaps even death, God can and will give you victory!

O God of love and life, help us to ever trust in you and give ourselves for you. In Jesus' name. Amen.

———«o/o/o»———

True Friends

Some friends play at friendship
but a true friend sticks closer than one's nearest kin.
(Proverbs 18:24, NRSV)

I had a circle meeting at my house this afternoon and needed to put the extra leaf in the dining table to make it large enough to seat everyone. The table is very heavy and I am very old, and I worked a long time to try and do it by myself. I tugged and pulled, but it was no use. I couldn't do it alone—I needed another to help. My good friend came to my rescue, and together we did it easily. That's the way it is with friends. By helping each other the load is lightened and the joys doubled.

We need friends in order to survive these days. I've read there wouldn't be so many suicides if young people in trouble had even one special friend who would love them and accept them. We all need to know there is someone who loves us and accepts us just the way we are, someone who believes in us and is there for us. As Christians, we know Jesus is such a friend and that he sticks closer than a brother. We will never be alone when he is in our lives.

But many people do not know Jesus or have him in their lives. Until they do, we need to be the kind of friend who will radiate God's love and let the Lord love them through us. It isn't easy to be a true friend. It takes commitment and a willingness to put the other's welfare above your own.

Every morning I thank God all over again for the friends he has put in my life and who have pointed me to God by their love and example. I pray I might be that kind of friend to someone else.

Dear God, you are my Creator, and I worship you with my life. But perhaps more importantly, you are my friend. I can be who I am with you, and you love me anyway. Use me, Lord, to give your love to someone else. Use my words, my deeds, my faith—as frail as they may be—to draw others to you. Isn't that what friends are for? In the name of him who showed us how to love as a friend who would lay down his life. Amen.

MARJORIE HARRINGTON

Trust and Obey

So the disciples did as Jesus had directed them, and they prepared the Passover meal. (Matthew 26:19, NRSV)

Some years ago, when I was in my early seventies, I said to my daughter, Rosalind, "I hope that when the Lord wants me to quit driving, he'll show me in some way."

One November evening in 1999, I attended a meeting of our church's nominating committee. As I left the church, I got into the driver's seat of my Pontiac, turned on the ignition, and sat in the parking lot looking around at what should have been familiar surroundings but which frighteningly were not.

I eventually began the normally short journey to my home, but although I read the names of the streets, I could not find my way home—there were no familiar landmarks, no houses, schools, or churches I recognized as I cried and prayed for guidance. I had the good sense to stop my car.

Another auto with a couple of girls inside stopped alongside me, and one of the girls said to me, "Ma'am, you were driving so badly we told a policeman."

"Oh! Thank God," I exclaimed.

The young policeman was gentle, kind, and understanding. With his cell phone he called my daughter, who arrived within minutes. Leaving my car for her son to pick up later, she drove me home. Even then, although I had remembered her phone number, I didn't recognize my home until she persuaded me into the small apartment and I saw my own furniture and familiar knickknacks.

"Mom," my daughter said, "you remember once saying that you hoped the Lord would tell you when it was time for you to stop driving? Well, don't you think he's telling you now?"

I handed over both sets of car keys, and a new chapter in my life began. In the next day or so, my doctor told me that an MRI revealed that I had had a slight stroke. Then I knew that the Lord has issued me a warning—quit driving! The wonder of it all is that I happily relinquished my car, even though driving had been the source of much pleasure.

Do I miss driving? Yes, very definitely. Do I regret following God's will? No, very definitely. Accepting God's will brings its own reward.

Dear Lord, just as the disciples followed Christ's direction, help us to accept your will and your way in our lives. Amen.

W. KENNETH JACKSON

―――⟨ঞ/ঞ/ঞ⟩―――

Love, Power, and Fear

> For God did not give us a spirit of cowardice, but
> rather a spirit of power and of love and of self-disci-
> pline. (2 Timothy 1:7, NRSV)

A very wise man once said, "The greatest thing you will
ever learn is just to love and be loved in return." To that I
would add, "and to learn that God loves you."

I learned about love early in life. My siblings (four
brothers and four sisters) and I saw total and complete love
between our mother and father. They dedicated their lives
to each other and to rearing their children.

I was born in Illinois, the fourth child of a farm boy
who grew up to become a Methodist minister. Tuberculosis was common in Illinois, and my mother was not well.
So my dad decided to move to Colorado, where there
would be no fear of tuberculosis. My mother's health

improved greatly, and she lived to the age of ninety-one.

In Colorado Dad served as an interim pastor at a Methodist church in the small mountain town of Beulah. After a few months he gave up being a pastor of any church. In later years he said that one of the reasons that he did this was because in Illinois he had had to conduct the funeral for three small sisters who died of food poisoning. He was an emotional man, and I am sure that was very difficult for him. I believe that Dad would have been able to continue his life as a minister if he had used the full power that God gives to each of us. I doubt that any of us use the tremendous power that God offers us or even become aware of it before the end of our lives, but it is there for the taking.

We need always to be aware that God has not given us the spirit of fear. No matter what circumstances we find ourselves bound up in, we should learn to have no fear. God will take care of us—if we will just believe.

Dear Father, may I always remain aware of the love, power, and spirit to have no fear. Amen.

———◦◦◦———

Mom in Ministry

She opens her mouth with wisdom,
and the teaching of kindness is on her tongue.

Her children rise up and call her happy.
(Proverbs 31:26,28, NSRV)

"I have a ministry too, you know," my mother proudly told me. At eighty-two she was still able to drive, while most of her friends and cousin-peers were not. Her ministry? To drive others to their doctors' appointments or food shopping if need be. Being able to help others when they needed help meant a great deal to her.

However, the time has come when arthritis has made walking much more difficult for her. Though she is not able to be with her friends and cousins physically, she has learned that what was of the most significance was not her providing transportation for them but rather her providing a listening ear, a sympathetic response, an unction to be courageous or an encouragement that they would likely not have had otherwise. As she laughs with them, cries with them, listens to them, and shares with them, Mom maintains her real ministry—to the hearts of those folks with whom she stays in close contact daily by telephone.

As Mom, like myself, is a Jewish believer in Jesus, she is the only touch of the Lord most of those fellow Jewish folks ever have. Her ministry now? To be the word and love of the Lord, a touch of the God of Abraham, Isaac, and Jacob himself to these dear ones.

As I consider my own golden years I have before me the best of role models, my mom, a woman in ministry where it matters most, in the hearts of the people in our daily lives.

God of Israel, God of all, help me today and every day have eyes to see and ears to hear the ones you put in my life that you want to minister to and help me to respond to them as you would. Amen.

Fair Meeks

Eyes Wide Open

Open my eyes, so that I may behold wondrous things.
(Psalm 119:18, NRSV)

Yesterday the doctor told me I have cataracts. Not just in one eye, but in both. "No," I protested. "Cataracts belong to—old people! And at seventy-plus I'm not old! I don't need surgery yet, but it's definitely in the future.

Just as I was about to throw a big pity party, a strange thing happened. The doctor put in some drops to dilate my eyes, and suddenly I could see better. He explained that the wider pupils let in more light so that I could see better around the cataracts. More light made it possible to see around and past the obstacles.

As we age, there are so many obstacles that appear in our line of sight: arthritis, cancer, that little heart murmur, failing memory. It's possible to focus just on those obstacles, especially since they keep us from our former energies and activities. We even assume that our personal obstacle excuses us from participation in his kingdom. This kind of focus is really spiritual shortsightedness.

The light of God, on the other hand, can change our perceptions so that we can see him beyond and around all these things. The cataracts seem oppressive, stultifying, even blinding, and yet discovery of them gives us still another opportunity to focus on God and his will for us, and with James we can see even this as nothing but joy.

Loving Father, continue to open my mind that I may be able to praise you for the blessings you pour out on me daily. Open my eyes that I may see the wonderful things you give me, and open my heart that I may grow toward a vision of your glory. In Jesus' name. Amen.

—◦◦◦—

Light Your World

> Ye are the light of the world … light a candle and put it
> on a candlestick…. Let your light so shine before men
> that they may see your good works and glorify your
> Father which is in heaven. (Matthew 5:14-16, NCV)

Growing up in rural central Louisiana, my world was
small. And since there was no electricity, my world was
also very dark. As I walked home from church in the darkness, a bush became a creature ready to attack and the snap
of a twig became the signal to run as fast as my skinny little legs would allow.

Years later my husband, our four sons, and I went into
a cave in northern Arkansas. The guide turned the light
off. Never before had I felt such darkness. After a long
thirty seconds, I told the guide, "You can turn the light
back on." My family was totally embarrassed and others in

the group totally amused. However, no one objected to my suggestion.

I much prefer sunshine, laughter, and vibrant colors. I enjoy light! In those times of utter darkness, light becomes a beacon of hope.

Yet there are times I willfully walk in darkness, the darkness of fear, the darkness of the unknown, and the darkness of sin. There have been times in my spiritual walk when the darkness has been heavy and oppressing, much like the darkness in the cave. The two agonizing years of my husband's mental illness and his sudden death were extremely difficult and dark. During those dark days and even darker nights, I yearned for light, a ray of sunshine, a bright smile, a touch, a thoughtful act. And I cried out to God, "Where are you?" During that dark time God did send a sliver of light that gave birth to hope. He said, "Be still, and know that I am God" (Psalm 46:10, NRSV).

When other people didn't know how to respond to my situation, God's Word continued to be a source of light and comfort to me.

We live in a dark, hurting world. In the dark, pain is intensified, problems are magnified, and loneliness is unbearable. Darkness is cold and isolating.

King David must have gone through some dark days, for he said in Psalm 18:28 (KJV), "For thou wilt light my candle; the Lord my God will enlighten my darkness."

It is amazing what one lighted candle can do. It radiates warmth, love, and hope. In light, pain diminishes, problems are solvable, and loneliness is manageable.

Lord, you have illumined my world. Show me how to share your light with those in darkness. Amen.

Robert Johnson-Smith

——⟨∞⟩——

God's Amazing Grace

My grace is sufficient for thee: for my strength is
made perfect in weakness. (2 Corinthians 12:9, KJV)

Most of us come to times in our lives when we ask questions and yearn for answers to our questions. *Paul,* the flaming herald of Calvary's tidings, prayed to God when he was troubled by a thorn in his flesh. He described it as a messenger of Satan that buffeted him from time to time. He prayed to God and asked God to remove the thorn. God answered his prayer, but he did not remove the thorn. God gave Paul the assurance that no matter what happened to him, God's grace would be sufficient for him to do God's work even with a thorn.

Paul lived a great life of service to God and humanity. He kept the thorn, but God's grace made it possible for him to do great things for God and humankind even with the thorn. Some scholars contend that *Paul's* influence on the growth of the Christian church in the first century was second only to that of Jesus Christ.

When Paul was near the end of his life, he was arrested and confined to the death row of a Roman jail. He requested and was granted permission to write one letter before his execution. He wrote his last letter to Timothy, one of his sons in the ministry. He requested Timothy to come see him as soon as possible because he was on death row. He stated to Timothy some things he wanted him to know in the event he was executed before Timothy got to the Roman jail. Paul wrote to Timothy, "For I am now ready to be offered, and the time of my departure is at hand. I have fought a good fight, I have finished my course, I have kept the faith" (2 Timothy 4:6-7, KJV). It seems to me that this was Paul's way of saying that God's grace was sufficient.

Over the fifty years of my ministry, I have known successes and failures, peaks and valleys, joys and sorrows, health and sickness. I know now that no matter what happens to me, "God's grace is sufficient for me." You see, God has the last word, and that word is good.

As you read the words of this brief devotion, I do not know where you are in the living of your years. I share with you what I do know from my own experience. *God's grace is sufficient.* He knows how much you can bear. Trust him. God cares for you. God answers prayer. God can deal with the thorn in your life. God is able, able, able, and able to see you through.

Heavenly Father, we trust you in all things we do. We know that you love us, and we know that your grace is sufficient. Amen.

—⟨⟨⟩⟩—

Attitude Is Everything

I have learned the secret of being content in any and every situation, whether well fed or hungry, whether living in plenty or in want. I can do everything through him who gives me strength. (Philippians 4:12-13, NIV)

Yes! Attitude is everything! It impacts your physical, social, mental, and even financial health. While I was on a bus with a teen choir tour, one of the young adult sponsors asked me, "As a grandmother, what is the most important lesson you have learned in life?"

I answered almost immediately, "Acceptance."

She said ruefully, "I was afraid you would say something like that."

Acceptance is part of that all-important attitude. Learning that something positive can always be found in a bad situation; not allowing what some people would call a disability to disable you; and knowing that reacting to an attitude with an attitude can cause a lot of trouble—these are a few attitude principles. A good example is a Bible hero named Paul who wrote the Scripture passage quoted above. He had learned to be satisfied with what he had.

To be perfectly honest, acceptance is the most important lesson I'm learning. I haven't totally learned it. Someone has said that we really haven't learned something until we can teach it. The older I get the more I see the wisdom of an attitude of acceptance, and it gets easier to do. My prayer is that I look for the positive, not allowing any disability of aging to completely disable me, and check my reactions to others' attitudes. This example might be a way in which I can teach something I have truly learned.

Lord, I want to begin my day with an attitude check and end it with a contentment balance. Amen.

Barbara Smith

——◦◦◦——

Checking the Lists

I will pour out my spirit on all flesh;
your sons and your daughters shall prophesy,
your old men shall dream dreams,
and your young men shall see visions.
(Joel 2:28, NRSV)

"There are few good things to say about growing old," I heard her say.

"What?" I thought, surprised at those words coming from an attractive, well-dressed, talented, and successful career woman.

In the days that followed her remark, I made four lists, and I offer them as evidence that we who are hanging tight to middle age or who have only reluctantly let it go have a bad habit. Following the lead of contemporary print and broadcast media, we focus on the glories of youth and the disaster of old age. But check these lists and enjoy adding your own items.

The Advantages of Youth

Optimism and wonder, curiosity

Ambition, potential

Virtually unlimited diet

Virtually unlimited energy

Ability to have fun

Apparent improvement

Outside support

The Disadvantages of Youth

Lack of control

Lack of personal funds

Power of authorities

Uncertainty about the future

Peer pressures

Fear of failure

Parents' expectations

Advantages of Maturity

Flexible schedule

Extensive vocabulary

Time to read

No more parent-teacher
  conferences

Lack of concern for
  appearances

Gratitude for each day

Long lists of nonessentials

Disadvantages of Maturity

Increasingly inflexible body

Increasing digestive problems

Documents to read,
  papers to sign

More child-to-parent lectures

Clothes that no longer fit

High medical/insurance bills

Too much stuff to get rid of

Sure, it's tough to realize that your toenails are thickening and you can no longer reach them, and it's tough to have to give up eating onions and garlic and black-bean soup. But isn't it a blessing to have the right and the courage—and the seniority—to hang up on the telemarketer?

I want to suggest to my pessimistic friend that while youth may be as exciting as a night drive on a back road in West Virginia, there is a certain comfort in knowing that you're on the straightaway and headed for home.

Our heavenly and ageless Father, help us to appreciate the advantages and the disadvantages of each stage of life, and, as we pass through each of these stages, help us to grow in wisdom and favor with you. Amen.

AMY WASHBURN

———∞∞∞———

God's Hugs

The eternal God is your dwelling place,
and underneath are the everlasting arms.
(Deuteronomy 33:27, RSV)

February 1, 1996, seemed much like any other day. My husband had taken a job in another state, and I had stayed behind until the house sold. I was packing boxes when the phone rang. "This is the Army Notification Center. Your son has been injured in Bosnia and is having part of his leg amputated." No!

Bob was a second lieutenant with the United Nations peacekeeping forces. He was on a mine reconnaissance mission with eight of his men and a senior officer when he stepped on a land mine. The explosion knocked him down, shattering his foot and uncovering a larger, antitank mine, which he straddled as he fell. If his leg had touched that, it is unlikely that any of the ten men would have survived. Bob was airlifted to a MASH unit, where he received the Purple Heart; then to a base hospital in Germany, where his wife awaited him; and finally back to the States. After six surgeries and the amputation of his foot, he began months of therapy and adjustment to several prostheses.

These pieces of information reached me over the next days and weeks. But the initial phone call came while I was alone, with no family nearby. As I lay in bed in the nights following, I thought about that foot: the tiny one I had washed so many times; the little foot that spent so many hours running and climbing; the foot that ran so fast in high-school soccer and track; and the adult foot that had so recently walked the aisle at his wedding. I grieved for that foot.

And I wondered how Bob would get along without it.

God's arms held me securely during that time, and Bob felt God's presence as well. I came to be so thankful that his life had been spared, and I marveled at each new thing he attempted. Today Bob has completed his residency in prosthetics and is helping others adjust to the loss of limbs. He skis, plays softball, bowls, and rides his bicycle great distances.

And he is now the father of two little children.

I'm so grateful for God's presence in times of comparative peace as well as in such times of trauma. As I get older I can see God's hand in more of my comings and goings. Those everlasting arms call me to rest and be still, as I trust the remainder of my life to the One who has lead me in the past.

Creator God, we are thankful for the confidence of your loving arms supporting us as we face the challenges of each new day. Amen.

Velma I. Woods

———◦◦◦———

A Zeal for Life

"Truly I tell you, unless you change and become like children, you will never enter the kingdom of heaven." (Matthew 18:3, NRSV)

Shouts of laughter, squeals of joy ... another welcome visit by our two small grandchildren has begun. Their enthusiastic expectancy and ours fill the air as they tumble in and cry out, "Mamaw and Papaw, we're here."

Everything they do is an exciting adventure, everyone they meet is a newfound friend in their zest for life, and their enthusiasm is contagious. As I observe how they conduct their young lives, I see complete acceptance, unwavering forgiveness, a faith that knows no bounds, and a love that permeates everyone they come in contact with. I wonder if this is what Jesus meant when he admonished us to become like little children?

As we grow older and our daily routines change, sometimes it is a struggle to maintain our zest for living. Exuberance was rampant in a household where every minute was filled with helping children with homework, driving them to ballgames, and preparing meals to satisfy discriminating appetites. But when our nest becomes empty, we don't always feel the need or have the motivation to cheer each other on and to maintain an atmosphere of joy and gladness when the need for warmth and ardor is greater than ever. For as doctors' appointments, hospitals, and memorial services become more customary, it is easy to become depressed. When this happens we may fall into a pattern of disheartened resignation and lose our joy for life.

If your life has taken on a somewhat bleak routine and your golden years have become a little tarnished, take some advice from the greatest Counselor who ever lived, Jesus. Become a child again, laugh more, plan an exciting venture, make a new friend.

Dear God, show us how to become like a child, loving and laughing as a child laughs and loves. Amen.

Jan Chartier

If I Have a Choice

Your steadfast love, O LORD, endures forever.
(Psalm 138:8, NRSV)

I began watching how people grow old when I was in my late twenties. My parents were in their seventies and growing old very differently. My father denied and resisted the aging process at every step. In contrast my mother accepted her wheelchair with humor, grace, and dignity. Through the years I have seen many variations of those two patterns being lived out as I have watched friends, colleagues, neighbors, and others age.

I must have been around fifty when it dawned on me that both my father and my mother continued to live in me. There are times when I realize that my father's decisiveness and sense of humor are very much like my own. My mother's love and warmth toward people are also part of who I am. I could travel a path either more like my father or more like my mother as I age. That was a scary thought! I didn't want to grow old in a manner similar to my father's. My mother's more grace-filled approach seemed far easier for her and for those of us who loved and cared for her. I wanted so much to be like that.

As I pursued my wonderments about aging and me, I eventually gained deeper insight. My father didn't choose to have the small strokelike episodes that caused his dementia to worsen. By the end of his journey on this earth, he had changed so dramatically I had to remind myself who he had been to me as a parent. My mother's decline with debilitating arthritis was very different. Her thought faculties remained clear. Her emotional makeup gradually lost energy, but its character remained steady.

I have tried to adopt life patterns to keep myself in optimal condition, yet the aging journey is not entirely in my control. There is much I can do to exercise my body, eat in healthy ways, keep my mind alert, and stay socially connected. I can practice my faith disciplines regularly. Even so, the genes that led my father's family to struggle with strokes may well be dominant in me. Whether my aging path is more like my father's or more like my mother's, my hope will be in God's faithfulness. Think about this psalm:

On the day I called, you answered me,
you increased my strength of soul.

The Lord will fulfill his purpose for me.
(Psalm 138:3, 8, NRSV)

O God, I trust that you will fulfill your purpose for my life as I age. I am grateful for your steadfast love, which will sustain me whatever my aging path will be. Amen.

Life Begins at Sixty

> He led me around among the bones and I saw that
> there were many bones in the valley, and that they
> were very dry. Then he asked me, "Human, can these
> bones live?" I answered, "Lord God, only you alone
> know." (Ezekiel 37:2-3, NCV)

I thought turning fifty was traumatic. Then I turned sixty. And that made the blush of my fiftieth pale by comparison. For months after the little family party, and after the gifts and cards were all put away, I went into deep depression. To muse over the possibility of retiring in a couple years or of dying without completing so many unfinished jobs was definitely neither amusing nor helpful.

The church I was serving seemed to be doing well, so I put on a happy face every week. Deep inside I was struggling with fear and failure. Everything seemed to slow down at once, and all the aches and pains began to emerge—couldn't jog the mile as fast as I used to; was too sore after a little workout with the weights. It was a real chore just to get out of bed at times. I thought my body—along with soul and spirit—was literally falling apart.

Trying to reflect, study, and meditate on Scripture was no help, and that pushed my mind and memory deeper into unknown, uncharted waters. I spent hours pondering my problems: failing health, the lack of growth in my congregation, the apparent ineffectiveness of my ministry, my own lack of spiritual growth and academic accomplishment. I lost all joy for Bible study, prayer, and human relationships and had days when I prayed for God to take me out of my life and relocate me in heavenly places. But, thank God, he never answered that prayer.

About ten months into my sixtieth year, I began to see myself coming out of my dark night of the soul. Two things seemed to bring about my change. First, friends who themselves had known such depression kept after me through prayer and encouragement. Then the Bible itself came alive and became a precious instrument of healing for my soul. I rediscovered its deep message as I studied it and taught it to my students. That message had the power to restore and to redirect my feet onto a new and exciting path. I remember teaching from Ezekiel 37 on the dry bones and ending up racing around the classroom like a little boy who had just scored his first goal in a hockey game. "Can these bones live?"

Oh, yes, they can!

From that point on I vowed that my life would begin a new chapter, and rather than considering retirement, I would seek out new and challenging opportunities. I began to pray with confidence, and soon joy replaced sadness. I decided to start eating healthy (little fat intake), I put the sneakers on again, and I found delight in walking, exercising, and breathing. I started a new job counseling and teaching. I also decided to cut back my time at the church and refocused my pastoral ministry, while insisting on stronger lay leadership to fill the void. I soon began to get ideas for academic and creative writing. I finished the book I had started writing four years earlier and was delighted at the results. It was true: These bones could live again.

Dear Lord, keep on reminding us, gently by your Spirit, that today is the first day of the rest of our lives; and it often presents new and fresh starts to do whatever our hearts and hands find to do. In thy precious name. Amen!

———◦◦◦———

Life Gets Different

> My brothers and sisters, whenever you face trials of
> any kind, consider it nothing but joy. (James 1:2, NRSV)

Another friend has died. Notice I said another. To me, one of the most difficult parts of growing older is watching my friends get sick and die. Just when we reach the best part, life seems to fall apart.

In fact, sometimes I really get angry. It seems so unfair that a man and a wife, rearing their children together, working together to build and maintain their home during all those years of frugality should, just as they have the time and money to do things together, have that union abruptly terminated. Whether by death, heart attack, stroke, bad back or knees—why should the golden years suddenly turn to lead? I don't want to have my faith tested, I don't want endurance, I don't want to be mature and complete. What I want is . . .

When I get to that point, I realize what I am saying to God and to myself, and I stop muttering. But I don't stop resenting, and I don't stop wanting whatever it is that I want. How long does it take to be mature and complete? How can I be complete without those special people who gave life meaning for me? Doesn't God remember that I have only a few more years on this earth? Even recognition that I am voicing the same old questions that Job asked seems not to stop the questions or the pain.

Surprisingly enough, Job's answer means more to me as I get older. I know that I cannot understand the mind of God. Norman Dupuy once wrote that anything that our minds can conceive is not God. What I can understand, however, is Jesus' promise that he will be with me forever and that his Spirit will comfort me as I go inevitably toward my heavenly home. In a popular television show, a widow asked Jessica Fletcher whether things go better after a while. She answered, "No, they don't get better, but they get different."

Our pain and our sense of unfairness stay with us, Heavenly Father, and we need your undergirding arms to hold and comfort us. Help us to rejoice through our losses and our pain. In Jesus' precious name. Amen.

RICHARD N. BAIL

Practicing for Death

EPILOGUE

> Jesus said, "Abba, Father, for you all things are pos-
> sible; remove this cup from me; yet, not what I want,
> but what you want." (Mark 14:36, NRSV)

Death is not something of which I have been afraid. But on
my recent eighty-sixth birthday I realized that some preparation for it might be good. I thought of Matthew Fox's
reference to the peace that passes all understanding when
a good person dies well; I felt I would like to die well when
the time comes, calmly and in peace for the sake of others
as well as for me. I thought such a goal would be worth
practicing for, but of course we cannot die over and over
until we get it right. However, a light dawned at that
point—I realized we can practice saying goodbye to things
dear to us and see how it goes.

An opportunity to test that theory with a tentative farewell to something I cherished came with that birthday. For more than forty years my wife, Vivian, and I have loved the friendliness of the area around Rangeley Lake in Maine as well as the beauty and wildlife of the region. Almost every summer we have rented a cabin on the south shore of the lake. At first all of our three children would be with us. Later their places were often taken by their spouses or their children or friends. We were almost always there during the eight-day period in which both Vivian and I celebrate our birthdays and our wedding anniversary—our fifty-ninth this year.

Recently when we have been in Rangeley we have been going every morning to Fitzie's doughnut shop to enjoy local color along with our doughnuts and coffee. On clear evenings we would drive up a hill to view the sunset over the lake, after which we might drive through the countryside in the hope of seeing deer or moose. On Sundays we would attend church. Every few days we would take an extended sightseeing trip. Once in a while we would spend a few hours on the lake enjoying the loons. We usually cooked our meals, but often we would eat out at one of our favorite restaurants. When others were with us they would join in with whatever we were doing.

Sometimes I would take short trips into the woods from the cabin, but my favorite exercise by far was to take a long hike into the woods beyond the sound of distant road traffic. I might follow a logging road that was in current use, but an old one was preferred. A mere trail, including occasionally a piece of the Appalachian Trail, was the best. Sometimes I would bushwhack between roads and trails. I always carried a well-seasoned staff cut years ago. About five and a half feet long and strong enough to bear my weight, it was useful in crossing streams or testing uncertain terrain. At my belt would be a hunting knife and a canteen of water. Around my neck would be binoculars and a compass, and when not carried separately my camera and a heavy tripod would be attached to me somehow. I would wear a heavy photographer's jack loaded with waterproofed matches to be used if it became necessary to make a signal fire, topographical maps, spare camera lenses, a folded-up plastic parka, toilet tissue, and a coil of stout but light cord. I would see moose, deer, more bears than most of the local people have seen in the woods, a porcupine, a bobcat, partridges, spruce grouse, Canada jays, and other birds and waterfowl. I liked those sightings, but what always really turned me on was the sense that I was close to my fellow creatures and part of them.

This year we rented an additional cabin for the use of our daughter Carrie and her family, to which she and her children drove in their van on a Friday—her husband, Darius, came later in his Volvo. Our son Fred, on the first leg of his sabbatical from the University of Hawaii, borrowed their car from his brother Dick and his wife, Lynne, and came a few days later.

We planned that Vivian and I would drive to Rangeley separately in our car on the same Friday as Carrie, but that plan went agley, like Bobby Burns's best laid plans of mice and men. Our car developed an oil leak, and I did not dare to drive to Maine until it was fixed, which could not be before the following Tuesday if it was to be done well. So Vivian and I drastically pruned the list of things we had planned to take with us and rode with Carrie and the children after Carrie did a Herculean job of repacking and storing things on the top of the van. Fred would be at Rangeley, able to ferry us about and even eventually bring us back home if need be.

I thought that after our car was fixed I might fly home to pick it up and bring the things we had left behind, or that Fred or Darius might drive me home for the purpose. However, the second stage of the Experience was beginning, aided no doubt by the book about the Dalai Lama that Fred gave us for our wedding anniversary.

As the days passed at Rangeley it became clear that going back for the car would be mostly for my pleasure and would lessen the time during which others could enjoy Rangeley. I began to realize that deep down inside me I preferred to stay and come home with Fred, although it would mean four fewer days at Rangeley. It would mean no car with which Vivian and I could poke into back roads by ourselves. Not revisiting many familiar haunts. No camera. No walking staff. None of the books I had left behind. I cannot convey how much all those things I had come to look forward to every year, all year long. More to the point, I felt painfully aware that a year would come when I would say goodbye to them forever. I did not feel that this was that year, but I knew that considering our ages and other circumstances we might never enjoy them again.

But just as I cannot convey how sharp was the sense of saying goodbye, neither can I convey how light-hearted I was after deciding to stay. I felt as though instead of merely practicing, I had died and tasted a bit of heaven. I had learned that it really will be possible, and perhaps even enjoyable, to approach death with dignity and serenity. I hope through this little essay to share that learning, this lesson. And there is no reason it should end there—how about practicing liking that neighbor we have never liked?

O gentle, guiding God: Help every one of us to know that the aim of our existence is to align our wills with yours. Each time we let go of something of our own desire, we find we are that much closer to the perfect peace you offer. Give us confidence from our daily practice so that we might neither fear nor desire our physical death, believing that when that moment comes we will discover the unsurpassed joy of seamless unity with you. Amen.

CARRIE BAIL

A Tribute

Just a few months after writing his devotion, Richard
Bail Sr. died of a massive heart attack. His daughter,
the Reverend Carrie Bail, wrote the following tribute.

Though professionally Dad was a corporate lawyer, more
importantly he was a person on a spiritual journey. There
is much I could share with you about his path, as it was one
he and I shared frequently. As I prepared for Christian ministry, Dad was one of my greatest supporters and spiritual
friends. In my opinion he was definitely one of the saints.

After bouts with a heart attack and cancer over the last
three decades, he was learning to live very much in the
moment, striving to be Christ-like and peaceable. He was
involved in many pacifist global efforts, but he believed that
the most important point of change is within oneself. He
worked hard at forgiveness, releasing anger, and modeling

gratitude. He poured himself out for others, especially in the last several years as caregiver for my mother, who has dementia. Less than a week before he died, Dad stayed up most of the night at the computer making a Valentine's card that said, "Grant not so much that I may be loved as to love."

At his funeral, people did not speak of Dad's accomplishments or his intellect, both of which were considerable. Instead, one after another, they spoke of how he had humbly served them and cared for them.

Matthew Fox has said, "The peace that passes understanding is when a good man dies well." On the day he died, Dad taught Bible study in the morning (he'd been teaching himself Hebrew by means of a CD-ROM), made lunch, went shopping, cleaned, got Mom to bed, sent out his e-mails, then went to bed and died. Not a minute of suffering or worry or fuss. Just entrance into that eternal peace that he so long had sought and had written about a scant six months earlier.

Contributors

Caroline (Carrie) Bail grew up in a home with a global network. She lived in Mexico, was ordained in a Hawaiian church, and married an Anglican from Sudan. Having ministered in the United Church of Christ for fifteen years, she is currently serving the First Congregational Church of Williamstown, Massachusetts, and keeping busy parenting a twelve-year-old son and eight-year-old twin daughters.

Richard N. Bail suffered a massive heart attack and died a scant six months after writing his devotion for this volume. Professionally, he was an attorney. Personally, his daughter, Rev. Carrie Bail, says, he was an individual on a spiritual journey. He is survived by his wife, three children, and six grandchildren.

Margaret P. Bishop, a retired social work professor at West Virginia State College, resides in Charleston, West Virginia, with her husband of thirty-eight years, Arlen.

Catherine Patterson Bartell and her husband, Jim, have celebrated more than forty years of marriage. They have been blessed with four children, three children-in-law, and five grandchildren. Presently Catherine serves as an intercessor for the Catholic Charismatic Renewal in Milwaukee, Wisconsin.

Robert L. Bohon and his wife Lois have three children and four grandchildren. Robert plays the violin in a symphony orchestra and a string quartet. He also loves tennis, reading, traveling, genealogy, tutoring, and his iMAC computer.

Bernice Hill Borzeka is a freelance writer and is presently doing interview stories for *Judson Today,* the alumni-public relations magazine of Judson College in Elgin, Illinois. She was active in Christian education in her husband's American Baptist pastorates. They have two children and three grandchildren.

Nathan Z. Bridwell is a retired teacher who taught kindergarten through graduate school over a period of forty-five years. He has two daughters and two granddaughters and has been married to Helen for more than twenty years.

Charlotte Broyles has four children and ten grandchildren. Charlotte says, "God is working in my life. Each day brings a lesson on my spiritual journey of love."

Harriet Arnold Buttry spent most of her adult life as a pastor's wife. She pastored and worked as director of church relations and alunmi/ae at Northern Baptist Seminary. Since her retirement, she has divided her time between four interim pastorates and her family of four children, their spouses, and seventeen grandchildren.

Beverly Clark Carlson retired in 1998 as executive director of the American Baptist Historical Society. She and her husband, Allen, now live in Berkely Springs, West Virginia. They are the parents of three children.

M. Dosia Carlson is a retired United Church of Christ minister. She taught at Defiance College in Ohio before devoting a quarter of a century to ministry with older persons in Phoenix, Arizona.

Jan Chartier, with her husband, Myron, has served for more than forty years in American Baptist ministry. Presently they serve as a ministry team on the staff of Calvary Baptist Church in Denver, Colorado.

Myron R. Chartier has served in American Baptist ministry for more than forty years. Currently he and Jan Chartier serve as a ministry team on the staff of Calvary Baptist Church in Denver, Colorado.

William C. Cline is a new-church planter and retired Navy chaplain. He now serves as director of chaplaincy services for the National Ministries, American Baptist Churches,

USA. He and his wife, Libby, live near Valley Forge, Pennsylvania, where he serves as a volunteer on the historical interpretive staff at Valley Forge National Park.

Donald F. Clingan is a national interfaith consultant on ministry with the aging. He was the founding president and first executive director of The National Interfaith Coalition on Aging.

Jacquie Clingan, a licensed minister of the Christian Church (Disciples of Christ), retired in 1992 as the director of the Ministry on Church Response to Family Violence, Illinois Conference of Churches.

Luetta Cole, a retired first-grade teacher, taught Sunday school for more than sixty years. She has three children and eight grandchildren.

Arthur J. Constien is a retired Lutheran pastor. He is now executive director of the Association of Lutheran Older Adults (ALOA) located on the campus of Valparaiso University, Valparaiso, Indiana.

Jan DeWitt recently retired as vice president of program at the American Baptist Assembly Conference Center in Green Lake, Wisconsin. Now the newly appointed ambassador for Green Lake, she speaks at conferences and retreats across the country.

Frank T. Fair is pastor emeritus of New Hope Baptist Church in Norristown, Pennsylvania. He is married to Thelma and has four children.

Patricia Farrell recently retired from American Baptist Churches, USA, where she served as ecumenical coordinator in the Office of the General Secretary.

Beatrice C. Fuller is a retired nurse who has traveled across the United States and to Paris, Sri Lanka, Cairo, and Niger. She dabbled in ceramics and then settled on quilting, which she has been doing for twenty years. She is the parent of one son and one grandson, and has a dear adopted sister.

Vernette F. Fulop is the wife of Robert E. Fulop, as well as a mother and grandmother, a retired nurse, and a former missionary. She enjoys writing inspirational articles, cameos, and short stories. Her hobbies are reading, crafts, and traveling around the world.

Glenn W. Gill was born in 1931 and is a retired water pollution control manager and former biology teacher. He is an elder in his church and a frequent guest speaker who enjoys conducting marriage enrichment retreats.

Marjorie Harrington was born in London, England, and was married to a Congregational minister. She raised three children and remarried in 1980. She had a career in journalism and photography and writes a weekly column, "It Seems to Me," for the Great Bend (Kansas) Daily Tribune. She has four grandchildren and one great-granddaughter.

Grace E. Herstine has served as director of communications with the American Baptist Foundation for more than eleven years. She lives with her husband, Philip, a classical guitarist, in Phoenixville, Pennsylvania, and attends Royersford Baptist Church.

Linn Horn sees herself as a much-blessed woman. She is a pray-er, wife, mother, grandmother, and wanna-be quilter—signed, sealed, and (not too soon) to be delivered by Jesus Christ.

W. Kenneth Jackson was born in a small town in Illinois in 1917 and migrated with his family to Colorado when he was three years old. After graduating from high school he was employed in management for forty-six years. He retired in 1980. He has been married for more than sixty-three years and has three daughters, three granddaughters, and six great-grandchildren.

Nancy Karo Johnson is the author of *Adventures in Dying, Alone and Beginning Again, How to Introduce a Person to Christ,* and *I Have Decided to Follow Jesus.* She is in demand as a retreat speaker and preacher. She lives with her husband,

Emmet, in Mounds View, Minnesota. They have four sons and ten grandchildren.

Robert Johnson-Smith, now retired, was for forty years the pastor of Salem Baptist Church in Jenkintown, Pennsylvania. He is chairperson of the Pennsylvania State Human Relations Commission.

Patricia A. Kohls lives in Oshkosh, Wisconsin, and is a free-lance editor and published writer of devotionals and poetry. She enjoys giving workshops, traveling, camping, and hiking with her husband, Ronald.

Ann S. Kramer, a retired teacher, taught little children for forty years. Ann and her husband, John, have three children and four grandchildren. They live on the Oregon coast and enjoy ocean fishing and gardening.

Lonnie Lane, a Jewish believer in Jesus, is always amazed that he chose her. She has three children and eight grandchildren. She enjoys teaching and writing on the subject of the Hebrew roots of the New Testament, serves on the board of her church, and has been involved in church reconciliation efforts in the Philadelphia area.

Ruth H. Marstaller is the wife of Bill, mother of six children, and grandmother of ten grandchildren. She is a retired teacher now living in Florida in the winter and Maine in the summer. She served as president of the American Baptist Women of Maine as well as the American Baptist Churches of Maine.

Fair Meeks has been married for more than fifty-one years and has two children and two grandchildren. She has traveled widely and lived in Asia for nine years, including three years in China, where she taught under a Fulbright grant. She is now retired from Minnesota State University Moorhead, where she taught English and humanities.

Mary L. Mild is the director of American Baptist Personnel Services. She is also the editor of *Women at the Well, Songs of Miriam,* and *Worthy of the Gospel.*

Donna Miller was born in the South and has lived in Kansas for more than forty-six years. She has four sons and four granddaughters. Donna has served as a short-term volunteer missionary in Haiti, Thailand, and Burma.

Wilda K. W. (Wendy) Morris is a Christian educator, facilitator for interracial dialogue, and writer. She and her husband, Ed, have five children and thirteen grandchildren. Wendy especially enjoys writing poetry and is the author of *Stop the Violence!*

Stanley E. Mugridge is a retired American Baptist pastor living with his wife, Phyllis, in York, Maine. During his years of active ministry, he served churches in Indiana, Ohio, and New Jersey. In active retirement he has had a number of interim pastorates, and has served as interim area minister for ABC of Maine while still finding plenty of time for fishing, gardening, and visiting children and grandchildren.

Robert L. Muse was called to ministry while in the Army in Germany in 1960. He has served churches and colleges in Ontario, Canada, New Jersey, and eastern Pennsylvania. Currently he is an assessment counselor at Eastern College, where he received his education, and a faculty member at Princeton Theological Seminary and the University of Toronto. He is married to Carol and has three children and two grandchildren.

Wanda Naylor worked for thirteen years as the clerk for the Secret Place for Educational Ministries at the American Baptist Mission Center in Valley Forge, Pennsylvania. She was the organist for thirty years at the North Wales Baptist Church in Pennsylvania, and now, at age eighty-five, plays the organ for worship at Elm Terrace Gardens on a regular basis.

Gladys M. Peterson is a retired American Baptist Churches, USA minister having served with International Ministries as director of the overseas division. She is married to

Wayne and has two children and three grandchildren. She is active in the University Baptist Church of Austin, Texas, where she serves as chair of the diaconate and the mission committee.

Carolyn Beckner Phillips is a wife, mother, grandmother, and great-grandmother. After four colleges, four churches, and four children, she completed her college degree at the age of forty. She became an elementary school teacher and the director of a children's daycare center. In retirement she and her husband have been co-chaplains for the Towne House Retirement Community, Baptist Homes of Indiana, Inc., where they have served for more than eleven years.

Carol Spargo Pierskalla is a writer, photographer, and spiritual pilgrim. From 1984 until 1993, Carol directed "Aging Today and Tomorrow" for National Ministries of the American Baptist Churches, USA. The author of *Rehearsal for Retirement* and *Help for Family Caregivers,* she recently moved from California back to Minnesota, where she serves as a caregiver for her aging mother.

John H. Pipe was a volunteer chaplain at Craig Hospital and a church school teacher at Calvary Baptist Church, both in Denver, Colorado. He sings in a choir and plays in an orchestra. John is the father of four, the grandfather of two, and the husband of Carol. John enjoys travel, reading, music, and biking the many bike trails in Colorado.

Dolores Grandfield Rodgers sees her sixty-four years of life as a journey of surprises and drastic changes in marital status, lifestyle, career, education, and spirituality. She is grateful for one special person who became a companion on the way, whom she calls "sister" in spirit. Dolores lives each day and cherishes life with great joy.

Barbara Smith is a freelance writer, editor, and bioethicist. She is former chair of the division of the humanities and professor of literature and writing at Alderson-Broaddus College in Philippi, West Virginia.

Annie Schrader Spargo, with her husband, Jim, reared their three children in a house they built on Three Island Lake near Bemidji, Minnesota, in which she lived for fifty years. She taught high school Spanish and was the sole adult Sunday school teacher in her church for many years. Annie has seven grandchildren. She also enjoys reading, gardening, and her two great-grandchildren.

Ramona Tennison has fourteen grandchildren. She has authored six books; her latest, *Loving Legacy,* is a devotional book for grandmothers. Ramona is presently pastor of equipping at North Parkersburg Baptist Church (ABC) in Parkersburg, West Virginia.

Amy Washburn is a retired nursery school teacher who volunteers at the local elementary school and tutors adults in English. She has three sons and six grandchildren and lives with her husband, Howard, in Pottstown, Pennsylvania.

Velma I. Woods and her husband moved to the west coast of Florida from Indianapolis, Indiana, when he retired. They have two children and two grandchildren. Velma has always written poetry about her personal experiences. She also enjoys doing calligraphy, playing the piano, and boating.

Author Index

―∾∾∾―

224